The Path to Ananda

Swami Avadheshanand Giri

The Path to Ananda

A Mystic's Guide to Unlimited Happiness

First published by Westland Books, a division of Nasadiya Technologies Private Limited, in 2023

No. 269/2B, First Floor, 'Irai Arul', Vimalraj Street, Nethaji Nagar, Allappakkam Main Road, Maduravoyal, Chennai 600095

Westland and the Westland logo are the trademarks of Nasadiya Technologies Private Limited, or its affiliates.

Copyright © Swami Avdheshanand Giri, 2023

Swami Avdheshanand Giri asserts the moral right to be identified as the author of this work.

ISBN: 9789357761888

10 9 8 7 6 5 4 3 2 1

The views and opinions expressed in this work are the author's own and the facts are as reported by him, and the publisher is in no way liable for the same.

All rights reserved

Typeset by Jojy Philip, New Delhi 110 015
Printed at Parksons Graphics Pvt Ltd.

No part of this book may be reproduced, or stored in a retrieval system, or transmitted in any form or by any means, electronic, mechanical, photocopying, recording, or otherwise, without express written permission of the publisher.

INTRODUCTION

What is happiness? It's a straightforward question, however, there are as many conceivable responses to it as there are people in this world. Everyone seems to be searching for their i dea of happiness in their own unique way.

From a worldly viewpoint, happiness is often seen as a feeling containing a measure of health, prosperity, social status, professional or creative satisfaction, besides a loving family and friends. However, all these are transitory.

It is often said, lasting happiness can be acquired only when we finally leave this material plane and return to our spiritual abode. While this may be the ultimate truth, does it mean that we should give up on the idea of being happy until then? Or become resigned to our current state of being? No, most certainly, not.

Sages urge us to remain happy even amid this transience. They tell us to adopt a cheerful attitude and always smile instead of frowning at whatever life throws at us. The point is that we must work towards a state of being when nothing troubles us. This requires us to understand and focus on our fundamental goal and to have faith. Even scientific studies have shown that the source of contentment is not the active pursuit of happiness for its own sake but our attitude to life as a whole.

What brings us true happiness, then? Certainly, a clear insight into what life truly points at us, but above all else—love. Ultimately, it is our love of God and His love for us, which enables us to trust Him to show the way as He holds our hand, guiding us to walk that way.

THE ORIGIN OF TRUE JOY

We can be truly happy only when our soul is engaged in adoration or devotion to God. The soul is always tilted towards its origin, the Supreme, which gives it a reason to exist. The more we keep the soul away from its source, the Lord, which is its ultimate destination, the more unhappy it becomes. The nearer we are on the path, the closer we are to our home. Joy and bliss flood our being when we are on this path.

There is no true pleasure or happiness in the pursuit of worldly objects or worldly accomplishments. These are short-lived, fleeting and transitory because we are always in danger of losing them. If money gives us pleasure, we fear losing that money. If we have a lovely wife or a lovely husband, there's always the fear of losing this perfect partner. When fear lurks like an unwelcome guest, there is always pain and misery at the base of these so-called pleasures. Rather than pleasure, this causes us pain.

One can only find real happiness and pleasure in love and devotion to God. The more you build on and develop that within yourself, the happier you will become. You may find meditation boring to start with because our senses are trained to seek pleasure outward. So, we would rather literally move outdoors towards pleasure, run towards worldly objects and seek worldly triumphs. Moreover, we are so used to interacting and attached to each other that we do not find it easy to withdraw our mind from such attachments. Or attach it instead to the *Shabd* and *Nam* and turn within. Contemplation inherently requires effort to begin with and can seem daunting and unexciting. However, it will all seem worth the effort once you slip into the practice.

All of us must make 'Happiness' our buzzword. Go and get it. It's infectious, so spread it too. Let the pursuit of happiness be our personal agenda. There may be turbulence in the air, and professional and personal stress too. Still, focus on finding your precious moments of happiness that no one can take away, come what may. How is this done, one might ask. Trust yourself. You will eventually find your own route. You just have to try.

 This collection of thoughts will eventually help all of us find true happiness and motivate us to move towards our own spiritual growth.

1

MATERIAL SUCCESS IS ILLUSORY

Seeking exceptionally high standards of performance is a personality trait known as 'perfectionism'. Habitually, perfectionists can never fully meet their own exacting standards and thus they remain discontent with their accomplishments and, consequently, their own lives. Wanting happiness, perfection and satisfaction are always desirable, but believing that material success, in whichever form, is what will lead to satisfaction is both limiting and illusory.

The nature of the mind is such that even when you are in the most conducive environment, with the best possible circumstances that life can afford, you might still find reasons to complain, be miserable and feel empty. It is like unknowingly allowing a tiny particle of sand in the eye of our mind to distort our entire vision. It is almost as if you are seeking reasons to be unhappy and dissatisfied. In such a frame of mind, we will surely find the reasons too. To overcome this tendency, we must find solace in the time-tested dictum, 'Count your Blessings'.

The mind's craving for more can only be satisfied by an infinite list of things that will give us peace and happiness. How can we achieve this? Realise that the only place to look for satisfaction and happiness is within ourselves. Infinity is accessible only from within. Sages say that a person whose sight is turned inwards is always happy. This inward journey can be smooth and rewarding by the light of the wisdom provided in the Vedas and by the grace of the guru.

2

MANASA, VACHA AND KARMANA

Manasa, vacha and *karmana* are Sanskrit words meaning mind, speech and actions, respectively. The phrase is often invoked to suggest that everyone should aspire for a state where beliefs, speech and actions coincide.

The form of Brahman (absolute reality), the metaphysical fulfilment we should aspire to reach is immortality, imperishability, epoch and joy. *Paramatma* is the epicentre and the second stage in metaphysical culmination. The supreme personality of Godhead is the culmination of the Absolute Truth. The question here is, 'How do we reach this truth'?

Seers suggest we can begin by taking the first step of acquiring the state where one's mind (beliefs), speech, and actions coincide. This facilitates us in realising Brahman. The wisdom in Vedanta is not spelled out explicitly, and thinkers are always trying to unravel its true importance. However, spiritual wisdom cannot be acquired by intellect alone. It has to be received as a treasure of blessings and divine bliss through selfless worship of God.

3

POSITIVE THINKING

Positive thinking is synonymous with a joyful mindset. It means concentrating on the good in any given circumstance. This approach has a significant impact on our biological and cognitive health. It suggests that we positively approach both the right and wrongs in our life with the belief that eventually, things will go satisfactorily. Another trait to couple with positive thinking is determination, a passionate sentiment that implies persistence towards a challenging goal notwithstanding hindrances. Decisiveness appears prior to goal accomplishment and encourages behaviour that will help achieve set goals.

Therefore, positive thinking is akin to approaching life's challenges with a positive outlook. It does not signify sidestepping or overlooking whatever is bad. Instead, it means making the best of a potentially harmful situation, trying to see the best in other people, and viewing ourselves and our capabilities in a positive light.

4

BEING OPTIMISTIC AND SELF-CONFIDENT

Optimism should be coupled with self-confidence in our skills and capabilities. Self-confidence, in turn, implies that we know we can rely on ourselves and have a sense of control over our lives. It also implies that we are aware of our potential and weaknesses. People with low self-confidence often have a mistaken view not only of themselves but also of others.

However, self-confidence and optimism should be coupled with a sense of balance between time and labour. We must also surround ourselves with traits of spirituality that will heighten our enthusiasm and optimism. We should look to befriend individuals who will motivate us to achieve our objectives. Enthusiasm is infectious. When we are around people who are passionate about their lives and vocation, their zeal will rub off on us. And, of course, we must be enthusiastic about our spiritual quest.

5

LEARNING FROM THE SAINTS

In the company of saints, we begin emulating them unconsciously. They speak of our spiritual inheritance and show us the way within to help us return to our spiritual abode. They point out the way to this abode without putting us under any obligation or charging a fee. Could there be a better offer? Saints are ubiquitous, even though outwardly, they seem like one of us. They speak to us of other special worlds, the Creator, and our purpose in life. They educate us about the writings of spiritual masters and persuade us to experiment and investigate the distilled information they pass on to us.

Saints are love personified. They love not only their devotees but all of creation and everything around them. They look upon the entire creation with love and kindness. The radiant form of a saint may seem far away, but it is within us as well. There is a veil between us and this radiant form, but eventually, it will be revealed by our love.

6

THE LAW OF GOD

It is the fundamental truth that law and spirituality come tied together in a bundle. Therefore, one finds amicability and joy blossoming wherever the law sustains spirituality and wherever the law, although demarcated to protect and punish the person, is imbued with an understanding of the individual's concurrent spirituality. But what is this law?

Humans are made up of mind, body and another component that surpasses our mortal uniqueness, which we refer to as 'spirit'. Thus, declaring that the law bears no relevance to matters of the spirit is impossible.

We are bound by the flawless, auspicious, beneficial and adoring laws of God. We must have faith in them. The law concentrates on individual bodies while spirituality focuses on that unrecognised element that unites us. But they are interactive and mutually dependent because mortal experience is, paradoxically, that of being both diverged and united at the same time. Therefore, one finds agreement and joy blossoming wherever the law supports spirituality through unity or oneness. And wherever it, although carefully defined to both protect and punish individuals, is infused with an awareness of the individual's concomitant spirituality (unity or oneness). We must, therefore, live in the will of God.

7

THE PURSUIT OF SADHANA

Contemplation (*sadhana*) signifies a methodical discipline to attain a desired goal or knowledge. Sadhana is likewise done to make it easier to separate from temporal ties. A person embarking on such a practice is known as a *sadhu/sadhvi, sadhak/sadhika* or *yogi/yogini*, in Sanskrit. The objective of the sadhana is to attain spiritual realisation, which can be either enlightenment, pure love of God (*prem*), liberation (*moksha*) from the cycle of birth and death (*samsara*) or an identifiable goal such as the blessings of a deity in the Bhakti tradition. Sadhana can be done in various ways: through meditation, chanting of mantras with the help of prayer beads, puja to a deity, *yajna*, and, in rare cases, through mortification of the flesh or tantric practices such as performing sadhana in a cremation ground.

Instead of endless pursuit of worldly desires, we must make the best use of our time by undertaking sadhana. The end of contemplation—self-realisation—is attainable if we have the grace and blessings of the guru. It is in our hands to decide whether we want to continue being devoured by self-serving cravings, suspicions and restricting thoughts or to decide that we must set out to discover that there's more to life. We can also learn meditation, take yoga classes or do volunteer work for spiritual awakening. However, if the motivation is still 'What's in it for me', this thought could create boundaries for our sadhana.

8

PURIFYING MIND, BODY AND SPEECH

Experiences in life are vital for the development of the mind. Once you have understood these, you may engage in the field of action. Remember that karma is driven by volition or intention. So, the most consequential factor at any time is the quality of the mind or heart in the moment that action is instituted. When the mind has been trained through meditation to be sensitive to the subtle nuances of experience, consciously striking a blow against a living creature reveals itself as a moment of almost inexpressible violence.

Hatred manifests when one does not enjoy or desire something, forces it away by treating it as an 'other' and harbours a covert sense of anathema towards it. In addition to the many ways that hatred might show up in our actions, we also need to consider how it manifests in speech and thought. Right speech is refraining from speech that causes division or works towards separating one group from another while cultivating speech that builds harmony and mutual agreement. Even the most private thoughts can have an impact on oneself and others. When we inwardly regard someone as an outsider, this thought can reveal itself in various unconscious communication, such as body language, hidden intent and inadvertent rudeness. Purifying the body, speech and mind of hatred and replacing these with loving kindness is ideal.

9

THE GITA:
A SOURCE OF SPIRITUAL KNOWLEDGE

The Bhagavad Gita embraces the Upanishadic concept of Absolute Reality (*Brahman*) that marks a shift from the earlier ritual-driven Vedic religion to one that abstracts and internalises spirituality. It builds on the Upanishadic Brahman chorus, conceptualised as universal, unpretentious, constant, conclusive, ineffable and *nirguna* (abstract, without features). This absolute is neither a he nor a she but a 'neuter principle', an 'It or that'. Like some of the Upanishads, the Gita does not limit itself to the concept of *nirguna Brahman*. It teaches us about both the abstract and the personalised Brahman, the latter in the form of Lord Krishna. It accomplishes this synthesis by projecting nirguna Brahman as higher than *saguna* or a personalised Brahman. The nirguna Brahman exists when everything else does not. The text blurs distinctions between a personalised God and an impersonal Absolute Reality by equalising them and using the terms interchangeably in the later chapters. This blurring has led scholars to call the Gita panentheistic, theistic, and monistic, all at the same time.

Will we understand the transcendental spiritual knowledge revealed in the Bhagavad Gita by meditating on God alone? The Gita is a divine discourse spoken by the Supreme Lord, Krishna, himself and is the most popular and well-known of all the scriptures. Always revered as a true source of spiritual knowledge, it reveals the purpose and goal of human existence. Lord Krishna's divine incarnations manifest his supreme position. There is verification in the Vedas for this.

10

BRAHMAN IS ABSOLUTE TRUTH, CONSCIOUSNESS AND BLISS

Brahman represents supreme cosmic power, the ontological ground of being and the basis, intent, and objective of all spiritual knowledge. Many people inaccurately translate Brahman as 'God'. According to Sanatana Dharma, Brahman is said to be ineffable and higher than any description of God. Seers agree that Brahman is ultimately indescribable in the context of unenlightened human experience. Nevertheless, Brahman is typically described as Absolute Truth, consciousness and bliss (*Sat Chit Ananda*) as well as eternal, omnipotent, omniscient, and omnipresent.

Not only is Brahman considered the motivation for all that exists in the universe and the fabric of all beings, it is also mysteriously described as interpenetrating all non-beings as well. Even the human soul in Sanatana Dharma, or *atman*, is widely believed to be connected to or identical to the Brahman by followers of Vedanta. While this notion was first touched upon in the Vedas, it was later developed in detail in the Upanishads, which further encapsulates the wisdom contained in the Vedic texts. The whole substance of the world is present in seed form at the root of its causal tradition; the eternal superpower is its root cause. There is only one Brahman everywhere in the form of the spirit and other beings.

11

BRAHMAN IN VEDIC LITERATURE

Varying references to Brahman in Vedic literature, starting with the Rigveda Samhitas, convey varying shades of meaning. In these ancient Vedic verses, the idea of Brahman is the 'power inherent in the sound, words, verses and formulas of the Vedas'. Nevertheless, the verses indicate that this oldest connotation is never its foremost essence, and that this notion developed and grew in our tradition. The connotation of Brahman in the Upanishads develops into physical, ontological and soteriological melodies, such as it being the primordial existence that develops, supports, and holds within it the universe, the 'regulation of the world', the 'fundamental', the 'general, universal', the 'cosmic principle', the 'ultimate that is the cause of everything including all gods', the 'divine being, Lord, distinct God, or God within oneself', the 'knowledge', the 'self-sense' of each human being that is fearless, luminous, exalted and blissful', the 'essence of liberation, of spiritual freedom', the 'universe within each living being and the universe outside' and the 'essence and everything innate in all that exists inside, outside and everywhere'.

~ 12 ~

COMMUNION WITH THE TRUTH AND GOD

The flame must be protected when a spark is first lit to prevent it from dying. Likewise, tend to the spark of light illuminating the soul. A spiritual guru provides a protective shield around this spark through spiritual congregation or *satsang*, which means 'communion with the truth'. It is a congregation through which we can realise who we are as souls, whether God exists and how to meditate to experience these truths first-hand.

What are the advantages of satsang? We search for answers to the mysteries of life and death. We seek to discover if God exists, if there is a soul, if there is life after death and what will happen to us when this life ends. These basic questions lead us to explore spirituality.

But God cannot be encountered casually. It involves a process of withdrawing our awareness from worldly concerns to concentrate within. An unceasing number of worldly interests and desires pull our awareness outwards. Only self-control can withstand this pull that keeps our awareness away from meditation. To keep our attention spiritually focused, saints have given us the gift of satsang.

The literal meaning of satsang is a religious congregation of good people participating in devotional activities and services together. Satsang provides a sacred space where we can close the door to the world for a particular period to focus on our soul and God. In a satsang, people meditate or chant together. There are no distractions because all are meditating together. Sometimes, in a satsang, people listen to spiritual discourses to remind them of their true purpose in life. The sermons, introspection and spiritual charging of the satsang makes participants refocus their senses on the implication of meditation, ethical living, vegetarian diet, selfless service and communion of the soul with God. Satsang encourages us to engage in spiritual practices daily.

It also prompts us to participate in other beneficial activities. If we engage in worldly pursuits throughout the week, then satsang draws our attention to the spiritual side of life at least once a week. It is a wake-up call to people of all ages to spend time communing with God within.

13

THE STRENGTH OF WILLPOWER

Willpower is the ability to control one's own actions, emotions or urges. It is an inborn human trait that affects every area of our energy.

At the core of willpower is the ability to resist short-term temptations and desires to achieve long-term goals. Willpower is necessary to achieve goals and plans.

However, it is not always easy to muster willpower. You should keep in mind that it is stubborn and can help you only when you bring it to the fore with your own self-determination. Willpower can be equated with drive, determination, self-discipline, self-control, self-restraint and self-mastery.

14

WHAT IS SPIRITUALITY?

Spirituality encompasses the recognition of a feeling, a sense or belief that there is something greater than oneself, something more to human existence than sensory experience, and that the greater whole of which we are a part is cosmic or divine in nature. This acknowledgement of a Higher Power could be the result of following religious traditions. Or it could be the result of a holistic belief in personal relationships with others and the world as a whole.

It suggests that there is something greater connecting all beings and the cosmos itself. It also suggests a persistent reality after death and answers queries about the purpose of life—how people are connected, truths about the universe and other mysteries of human existence.

Spirituality helps us navigate our lives better. There are fewer struggles and less suffering when we behave in truly spiritual ways. We tackle waves of crisis with greater ease when we surrender.

15

GOD—OUR BEST FRIEND AND COMPANION

Association with the wise is crucial to spiritual development. The example and advice of a noble-minded counsellor is often the decisive factor that awakens and nurtures the unfolding of our untapped spiritual potential. We should, therefore, seek righteous persons as companions. People diminish by relying on those who are mentally impaired themselves. If you continue keeping the company of equals, you will not grow and stay the same. By relying on someone superior, you will attain excellence. Thus, we should rely on those who are superior to us. If we don't find a mature companion like a fellow traveller who is righteous and wise, then we should choose to wander alone like a king renouncing his kingdom, or like an elephant in the wild after deserting his herd.

Who could be our best friend then? Someone who raises our level of consciousness way above others? It can be none other but God. And who can introduce us to Him? None but the guru! Therefore, we should aspire for companionship with God. And it should be our constant endeavour to be with Him and be around people who always discuss Him and remain devoted to His discovery and worship. That is how we will reach Him and acquire eternal bliss.

16

THE SIGNIFICANCE OF MUHURAT

Vedic literature reveals that the odds of accomplishing a task successfully are significantly enhanced if they are carried out in an auspicious muhurat. A muhurat ensures that we execute a work in harmony with cosmic timelines for the best possible outcome according to our destiny. Hence it is essential to plan for a muhurat before commencing any auspicious work. Similarly, the auspiciousness of the day is vital for better luck. The days of a week are named after the planets because each day is said to have a certain planet as its Lord. The planet exercises its influence on that particular day.

This custom dates back to prehistoric times when units of time were quite different from today. Every Hindu ritual involves chanting Vedic mantras with a systematic approach to performing these mantras. This chanting, that is done according to the ritual or ceremony being carried out, emphasises on rhythm and clear pronunciation and is an important facet of Vedic shastras. Dharma further depicts the relevance of the muhurat. The Shiv Temple of Rameswaram presents a classic example. Lord Rama sent Hanumana to Kashi (Varanasi) to bring the Shiv linga, but interruptions delayed his return journey. Realising that the muhurat for the sanctification of the Shiv linga would pass by, Rama did not wait any further and sanctified a sand *linga*.

Similarly, we must think of the entire life in terms of its auspiciousness and relate it with God since it is an important attribute of His.

17

TIME MANAGEMENT IS ESSENTIAL

Time management is about determining what is necessary and allotting sufficient time each day to work on those essential things. Unfortunately, most people allow the most audible part of the task to grab their attention. Often, the shrillest demand is not vital, but because it is deafening, it fools us into thinking it is most urgent. One of the crucial things to understand is that how we spend our days is up to us. The team leader may ask us to complete a project by the end of the week. Complaining about the tight deadline with our colleagues all day is our decision. Instead, we could decide to sit down and begin work on the project and figure out how to allocate our time to ensure the project is completed on time.

Time management is also about deploying our assets in the right places. For instance, managing a sports team, like all management skills, is also about using the players in a way that ensures best performance. A good team manager does not ask the best defender to become an attacker. He puts the defender in the position that will benefit the team—in defence. Time management is similar. Good time management is not about leaving the latest class assignment until the night before it is due but starting as soon as the assignment is given. This will ensure we know what research is needed and how much time it will take to submit the best assignment possible.

Getting the job done for best results that benefit everyone is also a part of spirituality.

18

TRUTH CAN BE EXPRESSED IN MULTIPLE WAYS

Ekam sad vipra bahudha vadanti (Rig Veda 1.164.46).

This translates to: The truth is one, but the learned ones call it by many names or describe God in many ways. Look at all that we assumed to be the truth that later turned out to be invalid. What incidents meant something at that time but fizzled out later? Observe how our judgements are all just bubbles on the surface of the water. They aren't facts and have no substance. We have judgements and think that is how it should be. Later on, we think, 'Oh! It was just my judgement, but not how things really are.' Therefore, our imagination broadens, focuses and magnifies. That which broadens, sharpens and heightens our vision, is *swadhyay*. '*Swa*' means self, and '*adhyayan*' is study. Thus, swadhyay is studying one's own self. Throwing light on our own 'self' and examining our own 'self' is essential.

By this contemplation, we bloom, and our inner being is unlocked. Then we begin to understand everything: there is one light, and that is within us. Then we find the way, and the truth dawns. We acknowledge that which is in all the holy scriptures. Otherwise, just memorising the holy scriptures and parroting has no value. Sermons in the scriptures must be replicated in the way we lead our lives, and for that, swadhyay is essential. Throwing light on our mind, intellect, and on the events of our life is important. By just throwing light on the events of our life, we will learn how we are; what concepts we have; how limited our thinking is and how vast it is now becoming. It will make us aware of the methods we employ and how our behaviour changes, and of how our sense of belongingness is and how it transforms.

19

OUR MIND DRIVES OUR ACTIONS

Spirituality is a part of life. Empathy is the fabric of relatedness, and it forms the fabric of our ability to live in touch with life. True empathy is a state of being. When we live empathetically, we connect with a life lived at a level of conscious and premeditated awareness—awareness of ourselves, awareness of others, and awareness of an omnipresent intelligence of which we are an essential and involved part. We are becoming increasingly conscious of the strength and leverage of our unique minds and how it can influence our life. Numerous books and scientific studies have connected the science and spirituality of energy and linked it to the human capacity for conscious choice and influence.

Yet, the area of our lives in which most people struggle is connected to emotion. When we are stressed or highly charged emotionally, our emotions colour our perceptions, which, in turn, colour our thinking and eventually impact our subsequent choices and decisions.

When we tend to our lives analytically, we heed the brilliance of our minds. When we listen to our lives through our emotions, we heed the intelligence of our hearts.

~ 20 ~

THE FEAR OF FAILURE

Your child is ill. You may lose your job. A friend backstabs you. The stock market plunges. You break a leg. Or everything that happens is often attributed to 'Karma'.

Karma! Is that bad? Or is it grace? Regarding, His role as supervisor of our karma, the guru tells us that a father's measures to set his child right may occasionally seem far harsher than those of the law. The father seeks progress while the law looks for justice or equalisation of accounts—an eye for an eye, punishment for a crime, a reward for virtue, and so on.

We think and live in terms of duality. Such as hot and cold, up and down, good karma and bad karma. Although we know that the guru is the supervisor of our karma, we still believe in these opposites. We understand pain as bad karma and pleasure as good karma or His grace. Therefore, we plead for the guru's grace and for the good; we pray for the fortitude to tolerate bad and distressing karma when it comes. Of course, we secretly always hope to avoid pain altogether. Or hope that God will arrange for us to feel mere pinpricks rather than deep stabs. In other words, we relish the good and try to grin and bear the bad.

21

THE ESSENCE OF DIVINITY IS OMNIPRESENT

Speaking about God, we can start with the origin story and work our way forward as God, the creator, and the covenant maker. Or we can begin at the end and work our way backwards with God as the one with tangible and intangible attributes. Since we have a complete awareness of God in our scriptures and spiritual experiences, the latter makes the best sense. We do not have to act as if our scriptures have yet to be written. They already exist. God revealed Himself fully by becoming human through His avatars.

We already know one of the most important things about God: He is life. For this reason, He has come to save the world by giving it eternal life. Knowing that God is life, therefore, stands at the centre of everything. It reveals God's nature to us and explains why He has granted life to his creations.

22

EARTH—OUR INVALUABLE HERITAGE

According to ancient insights, humans have five layers of knowledge—the environment, physical body, mind, impulse, and the self or the soul. Our relationship with our habitat is our first level of experience and one of the most meaningful. If our environment is hygienic and cheerful, it has a positive influence on all the other layers of our reality. As a result, all our layers are balanced. We experience a greater sense of peace and connection within ourselves and those around us.

A close-knit relationship with our habitat is built into the human mind. Nature, mountains, rivers, trees, the sun and the moon, have consistently been honoured in ancient cultures. Only when we started to disregard our connection with nature and ourselves did we pollute and destroy the environment. We must re-establish our relationship with nature.

We live in a world where countless people have become uncharitable and enjoy making quick profits and achieving instant results. To achieve these, people think nothing of disturbing the ecological balance and polluting the physical environment. They also stimulate negative emotions on a subtle level within themselves and in those around them. These negative energies, expanded and compounded repeatedly, are the root cause of much of the violence and misery in this world.

23

MOVING ON THE SPIRITUAL PATH

We are created with matter and spirit. Our body is made up of amino acids, water and fat. But our consciousness or soul is constructed of delight, vitality, spirit, peace and bliss. Anything that encourages the spirit and results in more joy, love, bliss, imagination, kindness and zeal is spiritual. You may ask if spirituality can be both good and bad. In reply, I would first ask if there is a good doctor and a bad doctor. No! However, some medics do bad things. So, every field has some individuals who give it a bad name. Similarly, if some greedy people have given a bad name to spirituality, it does not imply that spirituality is to blame. For thousands of years, spirituality has been the guiding force behind humankind. Spirituality brings keenness and energy to life.

However, to appeal to people of this generation, spirituality should stand the test of science. So, we need a spirituality that is integrated with science. In the East, unlike in the West, there has never been any discord between science and spirituality. Scientists were never condemned by religion in the East. Scientists have been denounced only in the West and in the Middle East.

24

CONSCIOUSNESS

Consciousness is the sea, and all the perceptual and believing capabilities that we gather all through life are ripples, the frills. Consciousness is the very origin. We can't get out of consciousness just like we can't get out of space.

When thoughts enter our mind, they create ripples in our consciousness like a concentric ripple in a pond when a single stone is thrown into it. These ripples prevent us from seeing ourselves in the pond of our consciousness. The pond is otherwise calm, but when we throw a stone into it, we can see that the splash of the stone creates ripples that expand in the form of waves, and the calmness of the pond is disrupted until the effect of the splash completely disappears.

Similarly, like the pond, the mind is calm and still in its natural state; but when we start thinking in a certain way, a series of thoughts create a ripple effect and proceed to occupy the mind until it is still again or until we gain control over our thinking pattern.

… 25 …

BATTLE BETWEEN BELIEF AND EFFORT

We all battle between our beliefs and efforts, something that is characteristic of humans. We say one thing and accomplish another. Consistently, there is a difference between whom we want people to think we are and who we really are. How many of us act exactly the same way in private as we do when we're in the presence of others or at satsang? When we decide to take one course of action, why are we tempted to do something else that is at odds with that decision?

As humans, we have the body, mind and soul. We often hear therapists speak about 'mind, body and spirit', especially in relation to healing physical ailments. We may get the impression that if we can bring the body, mind and spirit in harmony, we will lead contented lives. However, this would be a misunderstanding of the real relationship between the three.

Reason and spirit don't benefit the body. Rather, the objective of the human body is to act as a receptacle for reason and spirit. It is the only form through which the soul can return to its original home. Whilst we remain in the material body, the extent to which we experience pleasure or pain depends entirely upon our karma.

However, we turn things upside down or back to front because our lives are driven by our minds. We relentlessly try to find happiness in the world but move in completely opposite directions from our souls.

26

THE DIFFERENCE BETWEEN ILLUSION AND REALITY

In this rapidly moving modern world, we are ready to function and entertain ourselves with things that are undoubtedly not 'real', yet we are always in pursuit of 'the real thing' to bring home in the end. We labour, yet often spend a lifetime trying to find the difference between delusion and reality, unaware of how easy it has become to create an illusion, whether through electronic means, virtual reality or through a chemically induced mind state. We haven't quite reached the stage where we have to work out whether the person in front of us is a hologram or an actual flesh-and-blood person, but perhaps we're not far from this state of confusion. But our difficulties are not just with recognising the differences between illusion and reality. We find it hard to know whether we are being manipulated by those around us who claim to be our friends. Are politicians 'unpretentious' or 'deceitful' in what they say? Reporters constantly question whether or not those in power have told us the truth. We long to know which of the two we're dealing with—the real or the unreal.

Where does spirituality fit into all of this? Unlike politicians, the gurus don't go out seeking followers or making elaborate promises. They call themselves ordinary and average. They are born like us, grow up like us and go through the same processes of life in whichever culture they live. They may lead a family life, earn their living and even play like us. Yet, they give a quiet but constant message that is both extreme and unexpected. They indicate that the things we are most confident about, including in our own physical bodies, are illusions. If we want to find reality, we have to seek it elsewhere.

27

LOVE WITH WISDOM

When love is coupled with wisdom, it leads to everlasting love. Without clarity and an awareness of who we are, love becomes a fleeting experience. When there is great devotion, we take total responsibility for any misinterpretation. We may express unhappiness for a superficial difference, but when we do not feel dismayed, we arrive at a perfect understanding. We are in a state where all troubles and differences slide away, and only love radiates through.

Usually, we get stuck in differences because we have lost sight of ourselves. We try to exploit and control the other person in the name of love. This behaviour is natural because when we love somebody, we want them to be perfect.

28

FAILURE IS AN INSTRUMENT OF PROGRESS

Like waves in a volatile ocean that constantly rise and fall, success and failure are continuous. This constant flow is reflected in our life too. Everyone has wandered through the darkness at some point, so they have learnt to appreciate the brilliance of light. To climb the next mountain, you must first come down from the mountain you are on, first.

Similarly, failure is an instrument of progress in our careers—at least it can be, depending on what we learn from it. Sooner or later, inadequate information and experience, besides poor timing, personality disconnects and other such factors will lead to inevitable failure. Learning to use these as springboards for career progression is the key because failure can otherwise be limiting if we see it as an adversary, rather than embracing it as a friend. We all fail; but it can be a stepping stone if we allow it to be.

In most cases, it isn't failure that holds us back; it's the fear of failure. We fear losing money, position or prestige. We fear that doors of opportunity will close. We fear humiliation, unemployment, and so on.

Most of our fears are unfounded. Though the experience of failure can be painful, it's rarely fatal to our careers. It's actually much like crashing a bicycle when we are learning to ride. We may be hurt and our pride may be bruised, but we can almost always pick ourselves up from a career failure, dust off and start the ride again. Fear can make us risk-averse but we need to be courageous and act boldly—we need to get back on the bicycle.

29

CAUSE AND EFFECT, ACTION AND REACTION

Human life is a precious blessing. Sages have declared that every breath is priceless and should be utilised for self-realisation. This world is ephemeral and evanescent. It is like an inn where visitors halt for the night and go their different ways when the day breaks. Our remarkable world is governed entirely by a chain of cause and effect, action and reaction. The soul, thus, remains forever imprisoned by the body. Its release can be affected only by the merciful intervention of a God-realised spirit.

Life has two destinies—man is at one end, and God is at the other. And the distance between the two is infinitesimally small. Thus, the guru advises us to travel within while we are still alive. The human body is ephemeral, and everything is uncertain. Good health or illness can come seemingly without meaning but always as per one's karma.

We look upon our bodies as our real selves. To the average person, the mind is not easy to grasp. And very few people have faith in the spirit. However, sages tell us that the human body consists of three concentric layers—the physical, the astral and the causal. The mind and the soul inhabit the physical body. All creation—the mental and material worlds, spiritual worlds and all the gods and goddesses—is to be found within the body. Within it also resides the Lord, the Supreme Power.

～ 30 ～

ETERNAL POWER IS ALL-PERVASIVE

The relation between God and us is that of a part to the whole. There is no separation between the sea and the waves. There is no contrast between the sun and its glow. And God is never unmindful of us, even for an instant. He always looks after us. We have never been separated from Him. He is always with us and pervades our entire being.

When we are childish and innocent, God himself cares for us. However, when we thrive in our intelligence and begin to infer and ponder, then we feel aggrieved. If we turn to Him and hold steadfastly to his garment, and if we don't let go of our hold of him, as a child holds on to his mother, we will be happy. If we beg of him and cry out, 'I am yours, whether dutiful or otherwise. I am in your lap. Where else could I go if I left you?' he will not forsake us. This should, however, be said with love, truth and simplicity. The waywardness of sincere children is always forgiven. The Lord also relishes love, simplicity and faith.

Continue to be a child of God. Do not surrender the rights of your precious patrimony. Know God as close and cognizant. Remember him as a living entity. Do this with devotion.

31

PURITY OF SPIRIT AND IDEOLOGY

Cleanse the chamber of your heart so your beloved can enter. The guru urges us to unclog our hearts of our passions and desires, such as bad habits, everything we are carrying from the past and our expectations and worries for the future. We need to empty ourselves to feel the presence of our guru and God within us.

Just as we truly want to welcome the Lord into our hearts, He too longs to be seated there. Therefore, He needs our love as much as we need his love. He is patiently waiting for us to welcome him into our hearts. So let us prepare ourselves to receive him.

How can we do this? We can always live in the divine presence by training our minds to obey the Master, by living the *Sant Mat* (teaching of Saints) way of life, attending *satsang*, and doing *seva*. The guru always emphasises that service with body and mind is the best way to channelise the mind towards the highest service—meditation. Selfless service helps keep our minds focused on God. In this way, we rid our hearts of anything gross to make room for him to be seated there. Very often, the Master (God) gives us practical advice and hints on how to overcome our weaknesses and live by his teachings. These positive steps further actualise Master's words at every moment. Our meditation will make us stronger. It will protect us and create a protective barrier against the distractions of the world.

~ 32 ~
ADVAITA PHILOSOPHY UNITES *JIVATMA* AND BRAHMAN

The Shastras explain their perspective on the oneness of *jivatma* and Brahman. They stress the similarities in the fundamental character of the personal everlasting atma and the Paramatma, using the example of space. When an entity is placed in space, it looks like the space inside. It is distinguishable from the exterior space. However, if the entity that compels the contrast is withdrawn, the oneness of space is unmistakable.

Sita and Rama jointly illustrate the oneness of jivatma and Brahman that is untouched as long as Sita stays with Rama in belief, expression and act. The jivatma can stay with Brahman if it is consistently steeped in him. However, if it gets attracted to the illusory world of Maya, it begins to seek objects or people other than Brahman. The separation of Sita and Rama happens only when Sita shifts her interest from Rama to the golden deer. This separation is exactly the plight of the jivatma when it loses its moorings because of the allure of Maya, and is forced to take a body in every birth. It then gets estranged from the Paramatma and lives imprisoned in the *pancha kosha sharira trara* (Pancha Kosha are the five sheaths and sharira trara means three bodies) that it takes as a result of desire and past karma. Each birth or your *janma* is a prison, not something to be wished for. Liberation from the body comes only once a person is self-realised. The Shastras also show that the Paramatma goes out of the way to free the jivatma and grant moksha, out of compassion. The jivatma's effort is limited in the form of meditation and worship.

~ 33 ~
LAW OF KARMA

The law of *karma* states that all actions have consequences that will affect the doer of the action in the future. The results of one's *karma* play out in two stages: *phala* and *samskara*. A *phala* is an observable or hidden development that manifests immediately in the present life. In contrast, a *samskara* is an imperceptible result created within an individual because of *karma*, which alters and impacts one's capability to be joyful or aggrieved in the present and forthcoming lives. The theory of *karma* often refers to *samskaras*.

The concept of karma guides our life. There are 12 laws of karma constantly at play, whether we realise it or not. When we create good karma in our life, there is a likelihood for good things to happen.

34

LIVING IN THE PRESENT MOMENT

Living in the present moment signifies living purposefully, mindful that each moment we breathe is a blessing. Being in the current moment is a significant element of cognitive vigour. The past and the future exist only in the senses. It implies letting go of the past and not hankering after the future. The present is ephemeral, and thinking intensely about an unknown future or our troubling past may cause it to slip out of our hands. We sometimes waste so much energy thinking about the past or future that we don't realise how quickly the present moment flies by. When we aren't present, we become a victim of time. Our mind is pulled both into the past and the future. It means living our lives consciously, aware that each moment we breathe is a gift.

The mind is such that it always dwells on the past or worries about the future. It runs in all directions, away from the present moment. The truth is that the past is gone, and the future is uncertain. The present is our only reality. If we were to stay in the present moment and observe our mind, what next thought would arise in our mind? We would discover that there are no thoughts and hence no image of who we are. We would be left simply in the present, where true joy lies. The instant we go outside this moment, all our problems begin to surface, and we start to suffer.

How frequently have we had dinner without really savouring what we are eating? There are instances when we have sat down to talk to our kids or partner without listening to what they are saying or even sat in satsang despite having told ourselves in advance that this time we will keep our eyes open and listen attentively. Yet, we find that we are unable to concentrate. That's because our thoughts are constantly elsewhere. Yet, everything happens in the present moment. Nothing will ever happen in the past, nor will anything ever happen in the future; it can only happen now—in the present.

For this reason, the guru enables us to practise meditation regularly and punctually. Meditation introduces us to living in the moment. It trains us to be mindful of being in the here and now. In this way, the mind cannot tempt us into ruining our present by worrying pointlessly about the future.

35

SHABD IS GOD

Whatever is spoken or heard is *Shabd*; it reveals the real nature of things and explains the hidden reality or mystery thereof. But in the terminology of the saints, the term shabd has a much deeper significance, quite different from its commonly accepted meaning.

Shabd literally means hymn, sacred song, sound, verse, voice or word. It is the basis of all faiths and sustains all the forces of nature. The life force is also its manifestation. Like electricity, shabd, whether manifested or not, permeates everything. It is the string that connects everyone and everything with God. In the philosophical systems (*darshans*), shabd is equated with the authority of the Vedas (the most-ancient sacred scriptures) as the only infallible testimony. *Shabd* is God and is a life principle.

~ 36 ~

SELF-INQUIRY

Self-knowledge is the beginning of life's greatest and most important adventures. It is discovering who we are. Self-inquiry helps us to attain self-knowledge through self-control and self-development. Its goal is to experience and realise the Divine Self (*atma*) within us. In self-inquiry, it is important to take stock of your qualities—your capabilities, weaknesses, strengths, talents and your darker side. It is only common sense that one cannot understand or embark upon any enterprise before making such a self-assessment. So, when we want to know ourselves, we should start by understanding what we are.

Vedantic teachings are all about discovering for ourselves what we are. It begins when we say, 'I am going to find out who I am'; who will find this out?

37

THE PRESENCE OF GOD

Answers regarding the mystery of life and death are never satisfying. We will always doubt their authenticity. We, therefore, wonder if those who gave answers to these spiritual questions through the ages were correct. The only satisfactory answer for those who want proof is a personal experience. Only when we can see the truth of what is written in the scriptures or described by saints over the centuries will we truly believe and have faith.

Spirituality is sensitivity or attachment to religious values or things of the spirit as opposed to material or worldly interests. Spirituality is not merely an intellectual exercise, it is proven only by first-hand experience. To attain this proof, we need to do more than just read books and listen to lectures. We need to carry out practices to experience inner spiritual truths. The process leads from the outer world to the inner world and is a step-by-step scientific experiment. A guru teaches those steps to see the inner proof of spiritual existence.

Spirituality is the substance of life. The dawn lights up our lives, illuminating our paths and conveying light to the twilight, bliss to grief and meaning to the unfathomable. The core of spirituality is service. As we go deeper on a spiritual path and get closer to actualisation and enlightenment, we realise that the divine resides in all. We begin to see God's presence in every person, animal and plant. Thus, the feelings of care, love, sacrifice and devotion we feel for the idol in the temple also begin to blossom for the entire creation.

38

DO WE REALLY HAVE FREE WILL?

Do we have free will? The answer depends on how we decode the question. Literally, yes, we all have free will and can make decisions on anything. Every day, we face problems that have multiple choices; we make decisions and act accordingly. For most of our lives, we exert our freedom of intention and take decisions that seem relevant at that time.

We have exercised our judgement since we were young and have always acted on the assumption that we have free will. The gurus point out that from the ordinary, everyday point of view, we do have free will. However, they also add that from a higher perspective, our free will is not so free after all. We, therefore, must understand their perspective and their relevance.

39

IN SEARCH OF REAL HAPPINESS

There is an interesting story in *Kathopanishad*. Once, pleased with Nachiketa, son of sage Vajashravas, Yama, the Lord of Death, offered him three boons. Nachiketa wanted to find out the truth. So, the last boon he sought was the answer to 'Is there indeed life beyond death?'

Yama said, 'Boy, do not ask me about matters of life and death. Even the gods are not clear on all points. Ask me something else. I will grant all your wishes other than this one.'

Nachiketa was persistent and bent upon finding an answer to his question. He said, 'O Yama, I only wish to know about the mysteries of life and death and nothing else.'

Yama tried to offer Nachiketa worldly pleasures so that he may change his request for the third boon, but the boy was steadfast. He stated that all worldly pleasures were short-lived and did not render long-lasting happiness. Therefore, he had renounced all desire for worldly pleasure and was hoping to win the Eternal with advice from Yama, the God of Death.

It proved impossible for Yama to change young Nachiketa's mind. Finally, he agreed to tell him about the mysteries of life and death. He said: 'The Self is immortal. It was not born, nor does it die. It did not come out of anything, nor did anything come out of it. Even if this body is destroyed, the soul is not destroyed.

'The one who thinks he is the slayer and the one who thinks that he is slain, both are ignorant. For the Self neither slays nor is it slain.

'Smaller than the smallest and larger than the largest, the Self is living in all beings.

'Knowledge about it can neither be obtained by discussion, brain power, or learning. It reveals itself to the deserving one.

'This body is the chariot; intelligence the driver; the senses are the horses; conscience the rein; and the soul is the lord of the chariot. The Self is superior to body, mind and senses.

'Greater than the individual soul is the enveloping super consciousness, the seed of everything in the universe. Yet more incredible is the Ultimate Person, who is the goal of our aspiration. Once That (Supreme Self) is realised, death loses all its terrors and the one who realises it becomes immortal.

'The path to realisation is long and complex, like the razor's edge, narrow and sharp. Therefore, there is no time to be lost. Awake, arise, exert yourself, and do not stop until the goal is reached'.

40

TRUTH IS EVER-PRESENT

Truth is described as 'immutable', everlasting, 'which is above time, space and individual', and 'which permeates the universe in all its endurance'. Truth is also infinite and perpetual. Many elucidations of truth by sages explain varied other facets of truth. However, anything that changes cannot be entirely true. For example, the human body is not entirely true as it changes with time and is subject to death. It belongs to the category of changing reality.

In yoga, truth is listed as one of the five *yamas* that are fundamental for all spiritual *sadhana*: *ahimsa* (non-harm), *satya* (truth), *asteya* (lack of avarice), *brahmacharya* (self-rule) and *aparigraha* (non-grasping or non-possessiveness). *Satya* is sometimes translated as virtuous restraint from misconstruing and distortion of reality in one's expressions and actions. The two fundamental human activities—telling the truth and knowing the truth—have a close relationship with one another.

When we tell the truth, we practise the essential spiritual skill of knowing it first. When we lie to others or ourselves, we blur the boundaries of the truth. Lying robs us of that internal ability to recognise the truth that we all naturally have and diminishes our ability to recognise it when we see it.

.

∽ 41 ∾

WE ARE ALWAYS HUNGRY SPIRITUALLY

We all yearn for exclusive time with our guru. The guru shows us the path to self-improvement. That 'completion' is the satisfaction of our appetite for his *darshan*. How hungry are we for that spiritual food? What does that craving feel like? Would we be able to understand it if we had it? Even in a worldly sense, we may not realise that we are hungry. We may feel out of sorts, have a headache, be a bit grumpy, and then discover that we have been working so hard that we have missed lunch. Then we eat and feel better instantly. Similarly, we may not realise that we are spiritually hungry but may know we are not happy in this life.

∼ 42 ∽

FINDING ANSWERS

Humanity is still searching for answers to the riddle of existence from the beginning of time. Who are we? Why are we here? Where did we come from? Where do we go when we leave this world? What is the true purpose of life? What is the meaning of life? These questions lie at the heart of our existence. They provide the impetus that propels us onto the spiritual path. Finding answers to these questions makes life worth living. These questions are founded on the basic assumption that we are all here for a reason.

43

DISCOVERING DIVINITY

God is within us, but we have to discover Him. Godly existence is within us, and when we draw aside the veils around this spirit, what is revealed is the godhead—we are God. The soul is like a diamond inside a block of coal concealed underground. The diamond does not know that it is not coal. Likewise, our soul is trapped in the coverings of mind and body and further hidden under the dirt of our ego, pride, anger, attachment and lust. Our true nature is the same as the Lord's, but we think we are coal. We identify with our personality, race, caste, education, job, and family.

Let us imagine a grand palace or a wonderful home that has been left to decay for centuries. The walls are crumbling, the ceilings have fallen in, and rats, mice, spiders, and snakes have made this dilapidated abode their home. Such a place needs a restorer and an artisan to restore it to its full glory.

However, the remarkable glory and essence of Indian spirituality and culture is that it churns out gods from mere mortals. The perennial divine stream in Indian culture removes the stains of worldliness and makes us divine.

44

DIFFERENCE BETWEEN MEDITATION AND PRAYER

The significance of seva is immense. Seva, other than contemplation, is a means to an end. That is why the guru asks us to undertake meditation as our key service faithfully. Even when putting in our soundest effort, we don't know when we will undergo any perceptible inner improvement because that is not in our hands.

The whole purpose of meditation is service. The objective of contemplation is to equip us to carry out what God allocates to us and not to envision, imagine or let our minds wander. In prayer, we always wish, but in meditation, we constantly receive. That is the difference between meditation and prayer. We pray because we expect something, but we meditate because we prepare to accept what he wants to give us. In prayer, we speak to God, and in meditation, we hear him. Therefore, meditation itself is a service. First, we have to clean the utensil, and then we have to replenish it. That is the reason why mystics refer to it as a service.

45

LIVING WITH OPTIMISM

Spiritual life is about living with optimism; it is about living with hope and faith. The practice of religion should be empowering. Through our spiritual practices, we join ourselves with our higher nature and are filled with the power of the Infinite and Eternal.

Optimism and persistence lead us to such determination that we make all that is possible to come true. This is how we live a spiritual life.

~ 46 ~
ABSENCE OF FAITH AND SELF-BELIEF

We hear about Faith all the time. It is defined as complete trust, confidence and reliance; it is the name for an unquestioning belief that does not require proof or evidence or for the doctrines of a religion based on spiritual apprehension rather than truth or allegiance to some person or thing. It can also be another word to describe loyalty or a firmly held belief or theory.

Faith is confidence in what we hope for and the assurance that God is working, even though we cannot see it. It is the belief that God is working on it regardless of the situation in our or someone else's life.

We can exercise faith, which helps us find peace, joy and purpose. It gives us energy, potency and peace, centredness, stability and devotion. It is a great wealth and a blessing. People have faith in themselves but don't know who they are.

There are three types of faith: faith in ourselves, the world, and God.

We need to have faith in ourselves. Without it, we are inclined to think, 'I can't do this. This is not for me. I will never be liberated in this life.'

If we have faith in the divine, we will evolve.

The absence of faith may lead us to harbour negative feelings like escapism.

47

TIME: A PRECIOUS TOOL

Time has a peculiar presence that we can't handle, touch or visit. We can't speak to it, and it doesn't converse with us. It is intangible. Yet it is a teacher, a silent one — and never has a word been heard from it. It confronts us without delay and has endless patience, almost to a fault. It has no irritation, love, empathy, indifference or other afflictions. Yet it is a healer. It watches all that goes past but never interferes or alters any of it. Despite that, it decides our fate. It gives each of us a part of itself, but it doesn't ever tell us how much of it we have.

Time is a silent reality of our life, similar to God. There is no life without either. Time and God are words created by us to recognise the source of life or life itself as we live and experience it.

Time is our intimate companion; it never leaves us. We seldom recognise its central role in all our thoughts and actions though it constantly finds mention in all that we say and do, simply because everything takes up time, sometimes a little of it and sometimes more. When the little and more add up, it becomes all of it. Our language is full of time. If it weren't, there would be no language or even stories. We wouldn't be able to communicate at all. Our dictionaries are full of words that, in some way or another, are expressions of time.

48

PRAYERS FROM A PURE CONSCIENCE

Sometimes, we may find ourselves in difficult situations that cause us to question our ability to deal with them, especially when we feel there is no way out. In such times, it's easy to feel overwhelmed and be overcome with emotions of despair. In such moments of hardship, faith guides us in the right direction, and prayers for strength soon put us on the path to happiness again.

A simple prayer to God is offering ourselves to Him. What is prayer as it is ordinarily comprehended? Our minds create desires, and we pray to God to fulfil these desires. We never explain to our mind that we should instead strive to adjust to the will of God. Instead, we try to explain that He should accommodate the wishes of our minds.

We are slaves of our minds and not of God. Let us work towards becoming a slave of God; then, there will be nothing to pray for. We have to submit to what He wants us to do. We should pray to Him to give us strength to face gracefully and boldly, whatever He wants us to go through.

Before making any moral decisions, ask yourself if your conscience is at work. It always helps to know what is good for us and to consider the results of our possible choices. It enables us to judge the decisions we have made as good or evil and accept responsibility for our choices.

49

SPIRITUAL GOALS ERADICATE THE EGO

The nature of our goals may be the reason for our frustration. For some, the primary goal is to glimpse the light within; for others, it is attending to the sound. For some, it is leaving the body; for others, it is reaching the eye centre. For some, it is seeing the radiant form, measured in terms of the 'stages' explained at the time of initiation.

Some think only in terms of the ultimate goal like liberation, which may make them feel that they are billions, not just millions, of kilometres away from such a stage.

In the materialistic world, in contrast, goals are always limited in nature, however extensive or enterprising the project may be. It could be about accumulating a billion rupees, a vast empire, an excellent starting salary, a quick double promotion, having a baby, buying the most recent gadget, and the like. It can be achieved, and reaching it results in joy and a sense of accomplishment, which inflates our ego. However, in a spiritual context, goals are always to eradicate rather than swell the ego.

50

INTUITION SENSES THE SUPREME CREATOR

All religious and spiritual approaches are grounded in faith, without which no belief system can ever exist. But can belief be changed into individual and deep wisdom? Developing an academic understanding is never challenging, but if we strip away the externals, what do we know of spirituality from our own experience?

We believe that there is God. Such a belief is a fundamental element of any spiritual faith or belief. We say He is omniscient, all-powerful and ubiquitous and accept that He is the creator of everything. But how can such a being exist beyond all description, beyond attributes and traits and outside time and space? This concept is beyond the mind's capacity to grasp. So how can we truly say we believe in Him?

There is no easy or obvious answer to this question except to say that there is a facet of our being—which we may call intuition—that senses the presence of a higher power. When we observe the wonder of the world around us, whether reflected in the perfection of nature or the spectacle of a starry and endless night sky, our intuition immediately senses the presence of a creator. It gives us confidence that we are not alone in the universe and that there is a greater being who surpasses the endeavours of humans.

51

DEVOTION IS ESSENTIAL

Devotion is a vital component for success in every field; it is also the result of a deep yearning of the heart for God. Once a saint asked Paramhansa Yogananda ji, 'Devotion, that's the main thing, isn't it, Master?' Nonplussed, Yogananda ji answered, 'It's the only thing!'

To be devoted to somebody or something means that the object of our devotion is of primary importance to us. Devotion turns an act of service into an act of love. It means continuously thinking about the object of one's devotion and always being ready, willing and keen to spend time and effort on it. If we can feel honest and deep devotion when we meditate, it will become so important to us that we will allow absolutely nothing to keep us from doing it. When we make devotion an essential part of our meditation, we will automatically organise our life around our need to meditate, and everything else will take second place.

52

KNOW YOURSELF

Let us discuss the 'self' before we deliberate on self-esteem, self-confidence or self-evaluation, by whichever name you wish to describe it. Learning about the self is the understanding or determination of one's nature or basic qualities. Self-esteem describes what we think, feel, and believe about ourselves. Self-esteem has a direct relationship with our overall sense of well-being.

Believing in yourself is essential for success, relationships, and happiness; this same self-esteem plays a vital role in helping us live a flourishing life. It provides us with belief in our abilities and the motivation to carry them out. It is responsible for us ultimately reaching fulfilment as we navigate our life with a positive outlook.

Self-esteem is not self-confidence which implies trust in yourself and your ability to deal with challenges, solve problems, and engage successfully with the world. Similarly, self-evaluation is crucial to our mental and social well-being. It influences our aspirations, personal goals, and interaction with others.

53

TAMING THE MIND AND CLEANSING THE HEART

If we have time to love our families, how can we not have time for what provides energy for all we do? We can easily find time for meditation which is the foundation on which we can build an edifice that allows everything else to run smoothly. When we meditate, we are simply doing as God has asked us to please him and to help him help us.

God offers to hold us in his arms and carry our burdens. We need to let go. Spiritual practice is about letting go of all that binds us to this body and world. Our challenge is to tame the mind and cleanse our hearts so we can patiently prepare to meet God whenever he deems fit.

54

IMPEDIMENTS ON THE SPIRITUAL PATH

There are several lurking impediments on the spiritual path. The intellect can be one and often is. Lack of faith is another dangerous obstacle on the spiritual path. The student slackens his efforts when doubts crop up. Another significant obstacle on the path, and perhaps the most remarkable one, is indecisiveness and lack of determination. There are different obstacles that a sadhak may encounter at various stages of their spiritual life. A sadhak or seeker is often tempted to slacken efforts when doubts appear. You must be ready for obstacles if you are on the spiritual path. But with faith, these can be overcome.

We could reason that living—as in feeling, witnessing, listening, tasting, and believing—is a process of acquiring knowledge without reading and writing. Life is a process of experience, in other words! For the moment, let us conclude that spirituality is like life. If so, we would have a point. We enlighten ourselves with what we experience via the senses all day, and in this way, we learn without reading and writing. However, according to the saints and mystics, we do not obtain knowledge of reality through this route.

Therefore, to comprehend the rational foundation for meditation according to the teachings of the saints and mystics, a good starting point is to recognise that our life, as we normally experience it, is not real. What we experience is an illusion we suffer from and a misconception with no meaning.

55

PERSONAL SPIRITUAL AWAKENING

We live in this world without a real idea of our roots and our true abode. We all suffer from the same affliction. We carry great restlessness and dissatisfaction within ourselves, yet the nature of our illness escapes us. Things only begin to change when we are lucky enough to come in contact with a perfect living guru.

The literal translation of *guru* is the 'dispeller of darkness (ignorance)'. '*Gu*' refers to darkness assuming the form of ignorance, and '*ru*' denotes radiance in the form of spiritual knowledge. A guru dispels all falsehoods and lights our way to some ultimate knowledge, a phenomenon indescribable by words. A guru refers to a religious or spiritual teacher who, besides having deep knowledge that can lead to moksha (liberation or enlightenment), also has direct experience of the Divine vision or grace, which has been assimilated into the guru's being.

Through the guru's spiritual, psychological and practical insight, instructions are tailored to the seeker's needs to learn and advance spiritually. The guru is many things to us—teacher, helper, and guide. His illumination and joy attract us, but do we really know who he is? What does the dreamer know of the awakened one? The guru's great gift to us is personal spiritual awakening. Who knows by what great good fortune we made contact with our guru! At some point in our lives, we knew that the message was clear. We realise that God desires that we should become spiritually conscious.

～ 56 ～

GOD'S GRACE IS ALL-PERVASIVE

What do we understand by the simple word grace? Does it simply mean clemency or, more specifically, God's mercy? A dictionary definition of grace is the unmerited and free favour or blessing of God. Let us put it this way: all of us, at some point in life, have felt that we were being given more than we merited or deserved. We feel that a lucky star and God are smiling and shining on us. We generally think this way when things go as we want them to according to our plans and wishes.

But what happens when things don't go as planned? Has God forgotten to shower his grace on us? Is he punishing us? Is he testing our faith in him? Many negative thoughts come to mind when things don't go our way. Although we don't know what's best for us, we still expect things to work instantly in our favour. When that does not happen, we become disappointed and lose heart, and the thought that we are being made to pay the price for our karma depresses us. Little do we realise that this period in which we may feel low and unloved is the time when we are indeed being looked after.

57

DIVINE POWER AND INFINITE ENERGY

Initiation by a guru, your spiritual teacher, marks the start of a wondrous spiritual journey. From time immemorial, the spirit, our real self, has been waiting for this moment to transpire. It is the awakening from an age-old slumber. As we progress, our consciousness expands, encompassing everything. Being allowed to engage in Shabd meditation is said to be the greatest gift that can be bestowed on a human being. The living master is not only an unparalleled spiritual teacher, but is also the personal inner guide of the *Shabd* practitioner. Achievements or results do not measure progress on this spiritual path because it is infinitely more subtle and is linked to the experience of love. That love has nothing to do with physical love because it falls outside the parameters of the physical.

Growing consciousness automatically implies becoming aware of the differences in our attitude towards things and circumstances. In short, our whole being undergoes a complete and radical transformation. It is a life-changing process that does not occur overnight but over a lifetime or even many lifetimes. The spiritual teacher, untiring in his generosity, has come to this earthly plane 'to bear witness to the Light'—to share the spiritual teachings with us. The guru's love for God shines through in the way the guru speaks about him. We are urged to live by his will and to accept whatever comes our way..

58

GOD FAVOURS THOSE WHO FORSAKE PRIDE

Pride or ego is considered the most influential of our passions and the last to leave us. The most challenging aspect of pride is its stealth. It has been depicted as a black ant on a black rock in the darkest of evenings. This depiction conveys its invisibility.

The guru often warns us that pride is so stealthy that even thinking we are modest is a form of arrogance. Pride is vanity and the understanding of the self, the 'I-ness'—not the true self or the soul. Pride is about maintaining the self that we are familiar with.

Pride is about self-interest and self-importance. It manifests in talking about ourselves, our achievements, experiences, successes, failures and family. It also manifests in us thinking that we alone are right and others are wrong. If someone offers us good advice, instead of assessing whether we should follow it, our pride steps in and we may question their right to give us advice instead.

59

A BOND WITH NATURE

We share bonds with our fellow humans. Similarly, we tend to cling tightly to those animals whose lives are entwined with our own. Many people rear and love animals and treat pets like family members. Pets provide companionship, bring joy to our lives, give us affection, and we happily share our homes, food and lives. Similarly, millions of plants that inhabit our forests, mountains, plains, farmlands and deserts matter not just because of their inherent beauty but because no form of life can exist without them. So, we naturally care about plants, too.

We try to comprehend nature through our minds because our concept of self is lodged in there. This sense of 'who we are' is constantly changing our thoughts, moods, desires and images that pass through our mind like a never-ending movie, according to our changing circumstances. These changes succeed in raising questions than we can find answers to.

If we turn to God for an explanation, he tells us that this mind-driven physical self, on which we put so much emphasis, is an illusion and that we will never find answers through reason and logic. All spiritual gurus tell us that we have an inner self—a deeper consciousness or soul, beyond the mind, reason and logic. Spirituality teaches us that we must first become conscious of this inner self before we can fully comprehend God.

God tells us to change the direction of our search. Instead of looking outwards, we must look inwards. However, the only concept we have of an inner being or self is created by our mind. To know what we are, we must understand what we are not. To understand what we are not, we must observe ourselves. Our image of the self is based on such factors as where and when we were born, who our parents are, where we live and what work we do. As we have seen, this mental creation is not our true self.

60

NO RELIGIOUS SANCTION FOR CASTE DISCRIMINATION

Reform is never an offshoot of anger or hostility. We need a compassionate approach, along with the wholehearted participation of the concerned parties. Peace and progress can only happen through reconciliation and reform. The scriptures do not support the system of caste decided by birth. Instead, they support a caste system based on professional and innate tendencies. Such systems are prevalent in all civilised societies and every culture worldwide.

We should realise that being born in any particular caste is not a curse and that religion does not sanction discrimination. Every Hindu must know that many of the sacred texts were written by Dalits. Historically, many of the revered rishis were Dalits. The Dalit contribution to the literature of Sanatana Dharma is commendable. For instance, the narrator of the Puranas, Soota Maharishi, was a Dalit. Rishi Shaabara, born into an *atisudra* family, was a highly revered scholar and sage. His commentary on the Vedas is a highly regarded reference book for the most learned Vedic scholars.

~ 61 ~

A PURE CONSCIENCE CAN CHANGE THE WORLD

What is conscience? Conscience is a personal sense of one's conduct, intention, or character to an obligation to do right or be good. The concept of 'conscience' is commonly used in the moral sense and denotes the inherent ability of every healthy human to perceive what is right and wrong. On the strength of this perception, one's conscience controls, monitors, evaluates and executes actions accordingly.

Everyone's conscience compels us to act morally in our daily lives, helping to avoid or alleviate the immediate suffering of others. In contrast, social conscience makes us insist on moral action concerning the wider institutions of society and to change or alter social structures and practices that cause suffering.

Conscience describes two things—what a person believes is right and how a person decides what is right. More than just 'gut instinct', our conscience is a 'moral muscle' that sets our values and principles. These values and principles then become the standard we use to judge whether our actions are ethical.

62

SPIRITUALITY IS THE PATH TO LIBERATION

Seers describe that the spiritual path is the way to liberation. They tell us to renounce or relinquish our identifications, attachments, desires, and ambitions and to turn inward. They suggest simplicity and that we own less, have fewer outer activities and be quiet and still. They give techniques for achieving this state, such as prayer, chanting, and meditation, to strengthen one's connection with the inner self. They teach selfless service and the importance of doing good in the world. These are universally true and necessary if we desire liberation. desire liberation.

63

RESPECT NATURE

The gross components of nature that include the sky, earth, fire, water, air, rivers, mountains and vegetation and all living beings are extensions of one principle. Therefore, nature should be protected.

Among them, the five basic elements known as *pancha bhootas* (*mahabhootas*) are earth, water, fire, air, and space or ether. They represent the physical and energetic qualities of the human body and the physical world. The ebb and flow of these five elements influence our physical, mental, and emotional well-being. When they are in harmony, we experience peace and good health. When they are out of balance, we experience suffering, sickness and unhappiness.

All natural phenomena and living forms are interrelated; the weather, too, plays a very important part in the life of humans and beasts. When things are beyond the grasp of the intellect, humans try in faith to appease nature by singing hymns, performing yagyas (sacrifices), and so forth.

64

NATURE IS ABSOLUTELY FLAWLESS

The strife, stress, and tension of modem life have made people immune to the beauties of nature. Why can't we enjoy the beauty of meandering paths, swinging trees, flying birds and majestic mountains and hills? The fresh air and scenic beauty feel like heaven.

Everything in nature is splendid and divine. Nature is an infinite source of beauty. Sunrise and sunset, mountains and rivers, lakes and glaciers, forests and fields provide joy and bliss to the human mind and heart for hours together. Every day and every season of the year has a peculiar beauty to unfold. Only we should have eyes to behold it and a heart to feel it.

To develop a balanced personality, we need to have a healthy attitude that can make us appreciate and enjoy the beauty of nature. There is no balm to soothe our tired souls and listless minds other than the beauty of infinite nature surrounding us. We should enjoy it fully to lead a balanced and harmonious life full of peace and tranquillity.

65

GOALS ON THE SPIRITUAL PATH

Most spiritual traditions prompt us to give away a part of our profits to facilitate separation from the world and boost adoration for God. Charity represents the love that is God by providing for others whose material circumstances make life difficult. Charity is not about the quantity given but the love we give.

What we find in practice is that even though we may want to give to charity, we find it difficult because we are attached to whatever we possess and cannot give it away. We do not see that charity brings with it its rewards. Giving away a part of our hard-earned income inculcates in us the awareness that we own nothing of what we possess.

Everything we think of as ours, whether family, friends, possessions or other forms of wealth, are gifts that have been placed in our care. If we understand this, we will develop a spirit of charity towards all life in our hearts. We can then enjoy whatever we have without being possessive.

66

IGNORANCE IS THE ROOT CAUSE OF UNHAPPINESS

Our real-life experience is always different from what we read in books. We start to see what looks like dichotomies and denials, and they often confound us. At times, we might even challenge our faith. The best-case scenario is that if we're doing our part by living spiritually, we begin to realise that the path is a puzzle and that we don't know anything. For many of us, this is both a shock and a rude awakening.

Gurus do all they can to rid us of our treasured illusions about spirituality. They help puncture our false beliefs about what we think we know and what we think meditation should be like. They direct us to an experience of the truth that we can only discover through meditation.

The guru tells us we can't fill our stomachs by watching someone else eat. The master's spiritual understanding and experience will not satisfy our spiritual hunger. He became a mystic through the will and direction of his Master and his spiritual practice. Obedience and love for his Master and dedication to his meditation, which was taught to him by his Master, add to it. Similarly, we will gain spiritual understanding only through our experience, which will come from our spiritual practice and meditation, guided by our Master.

67

OVERCOMING FEAR WITH FAITH

Many things can make us scared, such as distress, which can be both physical and emotional. We become alarmed in circumstances where we have no money and no resources. We are also apprehensive of shame, fear mockery from others, and are afraid of isolation and loneliness. We fear the unexplored, dark woods that hide a multitude of fictitious horrors. We are panic-stricken by death.

Our apprehensions are wholly due to the frail, spineless and weak nature of this human body, our mental aversions and our lack of faith in the Divine. We fear because we believe that we are in a world in which blind chance causes events to happen in random order, and in such a world, we are victims—liable to fall prey to chance and fate at any moment.

Fear can only be overcome by faith—through which we can make sense of a universe that seems to be characterised by randomness, chaos, and unpredictability. Our experience tells us that life can go on for many years in a reasonably agreeable way, and then suddenly, our whole world can turn upside down. Business failures, divorce, political unrest and all kinds of things can happen to wreck our peace of mind. Even when our lives are going quite well, we feel anxious about what the future holds in store for us.

68

REVIVE LINKS WITH GOD

Saints remind us that the only thing that counts in this world is our association with God. For some divine reason, we are spiritual beings going through a human existence that circles around the need to reconnect with God. One of the roots of the word *religion* is the Latin word *religare*, which means to tie or bind. It means that the purpose of religion is to revive our links with God.

So critical is God's actualisation that if we forget everything else and just recognise this one vital thing, everything will be fine in our lives. If we did a thousand other wonderful things and forgot this one essential thing, we would, at the end of our lives, have done nothing whatsoever.

However, the ultimate tool of remembrance is meditation, in which we engage in remembrance of God. By repeating names that are associated with God, we focus on Him. The practice of contemplation and remembrance helps us see the Light and hear the Sound that leads us back to the Lord, our true home.

69

LIGHT AND DARK ARE ANTONYMS

God, who created light, also created darkness. Light and darkness are antonyms. Similarly, education and illiteracy are antonyms. The Sun, giving warmth and light, is the giver of energy and life and is, therefore, idolised. On the other hand, darkness has traditionally been associated with the devil and evil activities. We can't see and know what happens around us in the darkness and end up feeling vulnerable and defenceless. Darkness in our world causes insecurity as familiar objects seem to disappear into the shadows of the night, making us afraid and uncertain. However, this fear is the mental conditioning that we impose upon ourselves. There is no happiness without grief. There is no love without hatred. There is no hope without despair. There is no gain without loss.

Life is an infinite cycle of balance between good and bad, right and wrong, happy and sad, high and low, sunset and sunrise, life and death; the list is endless. How we perceive this cycle of ups and downs depends on our mindset and attitude; it also depends on how we look at things. Nothing can exist if its direct opposite doesn't exist. Can we only appreciate life and find purpose in it with these elements?

When circumstances prevent us from defeating a difficult moment, perspective allows us to find meaning in it to understand the reason for difficulty in our personal life. Once we know that, we can learn the lesson we are meant to imbibe from this situation, and move forward.

Enjoy the good times and bravely face the challenging ones.

～ 70 ～

OBSTACLES PUNCTUATE THE SPIRITUAL PATHS

Once we embark on the spiritual path, we should be wary of lurking obstacles as we learn to transition from the finite to the infinite, from one level of consciousness to the next. As in every walk of life, in the spiritual life, too, there are dangers to be avoided. And obstacles to be overcome. We use the word 'obstacles' with reference to both the inner and outer world, physical and subtle objects, and conditions and situations that stand in the way of our spiritual progress.

Embedded in the obstacles on our path are specific physical and mental disturbances. These include moodiness, despair, nervous agitation, and agitated breathing. We must be aware of our limitations.

After choosing our spiritual goal, we must search for a guru to guide and accompany us in this ultimate life journey. They lead us by our hands when we lose confidence and reassure us that we are on the right track. In that sense, they are our best friends.

~ 71 ~

EGO SHATTERS SPIRITUAL ASPIRATIONS

We are raised to nurture our egos. Our ego is what demarcates us in this world.

We're usually told, 'Don't be weak! Stand up for yourself!' when we feel hesitant about something. Modesty is rarely associated with worldly success. We are taught to be pushy to get on in life, stand out from the crowd, and be proud of our abilities. This may be good worldly advice, but it's not valid for a seeker. We must recognise that in creating this individuality and differentiating ourselves from others, we are also isolating ourselves from God.

Ego is the most significant barrier in the path of spirituality. Attachment to worldly possessions and worldly entities is part of the ego. First, we look at things, and a distinct impression is created in our mind about them. Then we want to possess them. To possess them, we work hard. Then we find that we are a slave to them. For example, an eight-legged spider has woven its web happily, and when it has woven it so meticulously, it finds that it has become a prisoner of it and cannot escape.

Before turning toward a spiritual path, the ego rules our world, behaviour, and desires. We can get rid of this alarming affliction and achieve an orderly state of mind only when we become attached to the Word, that is, to Shabd. That attachment drives out ego and creates humility within us. This Shabd or Nam pushes out the 'I-ness' from us.

When we merge into the Shabd and fall in love with our meditation and devotion to God, this 'I-ness' is chased away slowly. We derive pleasure in merging and blending with Him. Thus, ego is automatically dispelled. Without attachment to Him, one can never be detached from anything in the world.

72

SUFFERING IS A GREAT BLESSING

Suffering and happiness are outcomes of our karma in previous lives. Suffering causes our focus to turn inward, to face those parts of ourselves we might otherwise ignore. Then why do people pray to God for help in times of distress, knowing fully well that suffering is imminent and predestined? Can misery be a gift from God? God uses suffering to develop us into better people: The idea sounds contradictory. A *gift* is usually associated with positivity and cheerfulness, while *suffering* denotes grief and sorrow. So how can anyone accept that there is anything good about going through pain and misery, leave alone being thankful for them? For centuries, saints have testified to the fact that suffering is a great blessing because, in one fell swoop, painful as it might be, God pulls us closer to Him.

73

SUPPLEMENTING HARD WORK

Achievement is the product of many factors and not just of hard work alone. We require the right opportunity, the right people to work with, and the right timing. There may be an element of providence too.

Hard work is looked upon as the secret to success. But is it enough to bring about the desired result? What does it mean to work hard anyway? There are other, more compelling factors at play. They include: working smarter as time is a non-negotiable, non-renewable resource and people waste a lot of it; cultivating strong relationships, too, is vital. No man is an island by himself, even when he wants to be; one has to overcome fear which can be a serious blockage to success. Besides these factors, one needs a compelling vision to understand that happiness matters. One also needs to be consistent and learn to ignore the cynics. Also, one has to realise that failure is a part of success. And last but not least, is the fact that success requires sacrifice.

74

DIVINE THOUGHTS LEAD TO SPIRITUALITY

Divinity is an expression; spirituality is an experience. Divinity is the divine quality, the blessedness or godliness, and the essence of the existence of every being. Spirituality is the path to divinity and the experience of feeling in touch with a spiritual being, such as a god.

Visiting a temple and reciting *shlokas* is considered spiritual. During worship, we praise God. But can we count such exercise as spirituality? No, because the soul is nowhere in the picture. We can't practise spirituality until we attain soul consciousness. Rituals, such as prayers and mantras, are the repeated physical gestures or activities that are used to reinforce religious teachings, elicit spiritual feelings and connect worshippers with a higher power.

Spirituality is the intuition that there is more to reality than the physical, more to us than our bodies, and more to life than work and entertainment. It implies that we can participate in that greater reality, not just think about it but experience it in the most direct and personal way.

Each of us has a specific capacity for spirituality, a small capacity. As a person lives for others, that capacity is stretched and grows, which is spiritual growth. No matter how small the capacity is to start with or how intermittent and partial its expression is, what ultimately counts is not the quantity but the percentage of that growth over time.

75

SELF-DISCIPLINE—BASIC TOOL FOR ACHIEVING HIGHER GOALS

How does discipline help while following a spiritual path? Spirituality requires tremendous discipline. It is a 'lifelong' struggle with the mind. Meditating for a few hours daily may be a difficult task. However, let's look at it clearly and remind ourselves how much effort and dedication most of us put into making a living, looking after our families, or obtaining a degree. Why, then, should we expect to attain self-realisation without putting at least as much effort into our spiritual development?

However, here, as in many other aspects of spirituality, let us not oversimplify what we hear or view from a narrow perspective. Most of us tend to equate words like discipline and struggle with effort but also with tension, stress, and fatigue. We think we should lead a relaxed life and meditate with a relaxed mind. Therefore, we must ask ourselves what kind of lifelong struggle we can undertake calmly. There must be a 'right' effort (relaxed, peaceful and harmonious) and a 'wrong' effort (stressful, tiring, and frustrating). We probably experience both, not just in meditation but also in service and our daily lives.

Where there is modesty, restraint, virtue, adherence to limits, and respect for practical limits of life, God's grace and blessings begin to fall there.

76

THE 'WAY' TO MEET GOD

A human is the most elevated form of creation, just like angels. Humans are made in the image of God. The Creator and all His creation are within humans. And they have been given the honour of meeting their Creator while alive. This meeting is the aim of human life.

The whole secret lies in the part of the head just above the eyes. The 'way' to meet the Creator is found in all humans. This 'way' is the basis of all important religions, but most followers are blissfully ignorant about it. They are content with rituals, ceremonies, reading of scriptures and prayer, doing charity, living a chaste life and working for humanity's social and mental uplift, endeavours that make them feel virtuous; after performing these actions, they expect salvation as a reward after death.

The 'way' is the 'word' in the Bible; the *kalma* of Prophet Mohammed; *Shabd*, *Nam*, *Dhun*, *Akash Bani* and so forth in Sanatan Dharma and the *Nad* of the Vedas. These words are synonymous and refer to the same fundamental essence—the voice of God—which is going on all the time within us. We have the capacity to hear it when attention is held within instead of allowing it to run out and follow the materialistic pursuits of the external world.

77

REAL JOY COMES FROM WITHIN

Deep down, we all know there is something more than happiness, something more enduring that goes far beyond those simple pleasures in life that come with the birth of a child, a job well done or the purchase of some new gizmo or toy. This happiness does not last. Soon we are off looking for something more to please our senses.

That something more is consistently pulling at our hearts and always leaves us with a sense of a vacuum. Oddly enough, there can be a pleasurable melancholy in that void because that nagging feeling reminds us that God wants us to come home. Real joy is superior to everyday happiness because the latter is based on the fulfilment of the senses or some material delight or connection. There is nothing wrong with that kind of happiness, but it is not the real joy that comes from within.

We all have unspeakable secrets, irreversible regrets, unkept promises, hidden requests, irreplaceable losses, unfulfilled dreams, an unforgettable first love. Still, life is about being happy regardless because four words can sum up everything in life—'Life must go on'. But how should it go on? We all agree that it should go on happily.

78

DIVINE TRUTH VS. WORLDLY FALSEHOOD

Just as real and fake currency circulate simultaneously, truth and falsity coexist. Those incapable of discerning the truth from a lie are living in darkness. They are like travellers in the night, ignorant of the direction they are going. The task of religious teachers is to enable people to distinguish between true and false. A jeweller needs to be able to recognise the genuine ruby and discard the worthless stone; a merchant must learn to tell genuine currency from forgeries. As a person grows in divinity, night turns into day..

79

DEVOTION TO THE DIVINE

In the Yoga Sutras, sage Patanjali said, 'Devotion towards the Divine brings the perfection of *Samadhi*. It makes your meditation serene and takes you to the perfected state.' However, we can't take credit for our devotion. We can't say 'I am so faithful'.

If we are devoted, it is a godsend. Devotion offers ample joy, profound passion and *siddhi*. Siddhi means that what we think, happens; and what we enjoy, happens; we endow somebody and that also happens.

~ 80 ~

THE ULTIMATE PURPOSE

Our first and most important responsibility in the world is to do seva or service. If there is fear in your life, it is because of a lack of commitment. The thought that 'I am here in this world to do Seva' dissolves the 'I'. When the 'I' dissolves, worries dissolve. Seva is not something we do out of convenience or only for pleasure. The ultimate purpose of life is to be of service. An uncommitted mind is miserable, while a committed mind may experience rough weather but will eventually reap the fruits of its toil.

When we make usefulness our sole purpose in life, it eliminates fear and brings focus to our mind, purposefulness, action, and lasting joy. However, such an approach may come with short-term problems. Poor people fight for food, while rich people share their food. Richer are those who share power. More prosperous still are those who share their fame. But the wealthiest are those who give of themselves. The richness of a person is indicated by the person's ability to share and not by what they hoard.

What does success mean? There is no question of success if you have nothing to gain. And there is nothing to achieve if you have come only to give and serve. Triumph has failure inbuilt into it. If something is supreme, there is nothing to lose. People running after success only exhibit their deficiencies.

81

PROTECTION OF THE RIGHTS AND DIGNITY OF OTHERS

The guru accords us with several daily challenges. He encourages us to meditate faithfully, punctually, and determinedly every day. However, he wants even more from us. He challenges us to focus, prioritise, be joyous and positive and not worry. Obviously, if we meditate properly, the challenges to our mindset will be easy to deal with. Conversely, with a mind that is focused and joyous, meditation comes more easily. These are two sides of the same coin.

Amid the world's pain, developing a focused, positive and joyous mindset is a challenge. One might even ask: Is it appropriate to be joyous when so many of our fellow human beings are starving, living in misery, and dying painful deaths? Do we have any right to be joyous? We all are children of that one God, and we all are equal in his eyes. Therefore, we should strive to protect the rights, dignity, and autonomy of others. That is the ultimate religion.

82

HEALTHY THOUGHTS SPUR POSITIVE CREATION

Spiritual focus, self-discipline and self-care are factors that lead to positive growth in an individual's life. Spiritual rituals such as meditation, yoga and prayer are designed to nurse the soul. Self-care rejuvenates the mind, body, and soul. Positive thinking is one of the most important of all spiritual tools. Spirituality is that aspect of life among humans that gives it its 'humanness'. It also provides meaning and direction to a person's life by helping to deal with the vicissitudes of existence. Little wonder then that it includes such vital dimensions as the quest for meaning, purpose, self-transcending knowledge, meaningful relationships, love, and commitment, as well as a sense of the holy amongst us.

That is why spirituality helps reduce the ill effects of depression and promotes energy, calmness, and flexibility.

83

REMEMBERING GOD

Faith in God guides us during our life. With help from the gift of faith that penetrates our life, we can build a relationship with God that is authentic and almost as real a relationship as we would have with a physical person.

Life is like a roller coaster. Sometimes we are up, and everything is right with the world. But then come times when our world suddenly turns upside down. It is in these moments that we tend to ask ourselves: Where is God?

Trusting God is easy when things are going our way. But when the going gets rough, that trust can easily turn into doubt. Before we know it, we blame God for all the misfortunes that have befallen us.

Why is trusting God in difficult times so hard to do? When we are going through a hard time, we are so consumed with our sorrow that we disregard everything else. Of course, it's perfectly valid to feel that way. But when we focus only on our grief, we forget that there are people who care for us. We do not notice the people who are hurting because we are hurting.

Our problems and struggles become the centre of our attention. We zoom in on these and in the process, magnify our troubles. Soon enough, we forget our blessings. We forget the good things God is doing for us because of the trials He has given us. Yes, God gives us trials. But, often, it's nothing compared to his blessings.

~ 84 ~

SPIRITUALITY AND ITS POSITIVE EFFECTS

Spirituality has many positive effects on health and wellness. Spiritual care has the potential to be a powerful intervention in patient care. Spirituality could encompass the rituals of organised religion, adhering to a belief system and having a sense of community and support. It could mean talking about our situation with a saint or a religious leader.

Spirituality might centre on a quieting, transformative, individual meditative practice. Religious or spiritual interventions have several benefits, including the reduction of anxiety. Mindfulness-based interventions help lower psychological distress, sleep disturbance and fatigue, and they promote a better quality of life.

Meditating, praying, or even taking a nature walk helps boost immune system functions. When we are in deep prayer or meditation, our fight-or-flight response goes off, and our rest-and-repair switch turns on. This allows our immune system to supercharge our whole body and is incredibly healing, whether we are under stress, have an actual illness, or are simply trying to prevent illness or stress.

Meditation modifies gene expression in immune cells to be less inflammatory. The practice can induce feelings of calm and clear-headedness as well as improve concentration and attention.

85

HUMILITY IS A GREAT VIRTUE

Saints are unanimous in describing humility as one of the fundamental virtues that goes hand-in-hand with spirituality. Humility-like devotion is the basis upon which to build other virtues. Where there is love and humility, all other good qualities naturally settle in, like cream on milk. Meekness and humility are great virtues; we must cultivate them consciously and do away with our ego and pride to make more headway on the spiritual path. The ego is that part of our mind that provides us with self-understanding.

86

THE DIVERSITY OF THE UNIVERSE

To become as nuanced as He is. Our denseness is a cloak that makes us blind to the divine as our inner, spiritual eye is shut. Unfortunately, we believe that truth can be seen with our physical eye.

The guru says that mortal birth is for a twin objective: to revive our spiritual essence, find our path out of the creation cycle, and return to be one with the Creator. This means we should aspire to know and be with God before death. Many fail to recognise that when we die, we do not automatically reach God's kingdom. The guru says that a cycle of reincarnation holds each person back to this earthly level of reality, lifetime after lifetime. Each individual's spiritual purpose is to exit that cycle and eventually reunite with God. Through His will, God brought creation into being. Through His will, God gave the divine law, the Shabd, which is the creative energy that sustains the entire cosmos and all the spiritual regions. This Shabd is the link between God's resolve and God's ingenious action.

~ 87 ~

A POSITIVE MINDSET

Having a positive mindset is an essential requirement for spiritual life. Entertaining good ideas, staying hopeful in hardship, and steering clear of negative influences complement the teachings of Sanatan Dharma and are necessary aids for reaching our spiritual goals. In theory, it is a perfect plan. However, from a practical standpoint, how does one stay positive in a world that is constantly steeped in negativity?

'Be positive' is the advice given to us all the time. It is a welcome reminder, particularly when mired in everyday life's karmic punishment. With a bit of reflection, we can look at the bigger picture, come to terms with our circumstances, and perhaps feel a little better about our possibilities—at least, for the moment.

As disciples on the path of love, a part of us can accept in a second that everything is good and happens for a reason and is ultimately beneficial. However, being able to apply this understanding intuitively, all the time while being buffeted by waves of excruciating karma is not easy—unless one has a positive attitude.

88

SIMPLICITY AND HUMILITY

A child is guileless. Its mind is still pure and unsullied by the world. Children live in the moment and harbour no ill will against anybody. The guru says that if we want to enter within ourselves, and desire to change our way of life, then we must become pure and simple like a child. However, we have wandered far from that state of clarity and piety because of our ego, which makes us see ourselves as separate, different, and better or worse than others. We have strayed from that simplicity and purity due to our attachments to people, possessions, and pleasures, a state of mind compounded by our intellect, which only leads us deeper and deeper into confusion.

There is one truth, one reality, one God and one Father. There is one way within each one of us that leads back to him. In this life, we have only one true friend, the guru here to guide us on that path of union with that one power, the Shabd, that created everything. We can practice making contact with that Shabd and treading the path to reunion with Him. We have to focus all our awareness at one point in the body, the eye centre, to enter within the self.

～ 89 ～

GOD'S LAW IS FLAWLESS

Have you recalled childhood games or watched small children in creative play to see how children periodically disconnect from the adult world and create their environment and reality, at least for a little while? What a great ability! Should we not try to repeat this when we take time to go into that special place within ourselves at the eye centre? Doing this sincerely and regularly in the way we were shown at initiation will help us gain a tremendous sense of who we are and where we belong.

We carry fabulous glory within ourselves. The Creator has placed his essence, the *atma*, within us. And every human being can potentially come into conscious contact with the Shabd resounding in the forehead. It needs initiation from a spiritual adept and then the firm resolve to set aside time each day to cultivate separation from worldly ties by withdrawing to the eye centre.

90

TREATING EVERYONE WITH IMPARTIALITY AND COMPASSION

We are aware of how valuable all creatures are to the natural order. We have seen their present state and the social effects of our actions toward them. On the other hand, the spiritual impact of our actions is far more nuanced. Saints and great visionaries, in every age, have provided us with the same unequivocal message repeatedly.

There is a perfect balance in nature. This natural, God-given balance in the universe comes from pairs of opposites complementing each other. Light and dark, day and night, youth and age, energy and void, and masculine and feminine are necessary for this balance and well-being of creation. Human beings have both masculine and feminine characteristics, and men and women together contribute to a balanced society.

~ 91 ~

ACCEPTING PETTY DISAPPOINTMENTS

A newborn yells when startled by a sudden noise; a child shrieks when its toys are snatched; a student may bemoan his performance in an exam. As teenagers, we may have hollered when rejected by our peers. As adults, we may have whined when we missed getting an outstanding job. Nearly all of us have undergone these dark moments at different phases of our lives. We are told not to let such things bother us. Our elders pacify us and advise us not to waste our tears over any disappointment.

As adults, most of us have seen and undergone many financial, marital and health challenges, among others. Many of us may have already experienced the devastating loss of a loved one. Therefore, everything else should seem trivial to us. Still, we allow ourselves to be disturbed by small disappointments when we should be able to accept them with patience and wisdom. More often than not, we expect everything to run smoothly with our health, relationships, and other areas of life. Any slight hiccup along the way leads to so much stress.

∽ 92 ∾

SPIRITUAL PROGRESS IS DEPENDENT ON THE GURU

The path of spirituality is wholly dependent on the guru, without whom the path would cease to exist. Some paths may have a living guru, while others are based on the teachings of past gurus. A true guru is mindful of his disciples' spiritual worthiness, having reached the highest domain of spirituality.

Finding the guru and, through him, God is crucial for a spiritual seeker. However, with our limited spiritual insight, gauging the spiritual attainment of a master is impossible for us. It is similar to a kindergarten child trying to assess the competence of a university professor. However, we can compare the attributes of a living master with those of past perfect masters. Through this and our study and research, we gain the intellectual conviction that the path shown by the guru is the right one for us. Then we can dedicate our lives to following it.

93

FIVE STAGES OF MEDITATION

According to seers, raising our consciousness to the level of our inherent spirituality may be our tallest task, but it should be the immediate objective of human reality. To pursue this path of God actualisation, initiation by a guru is paramount. The guru brings us the message that there is only one God, and we can partake of his vision during our lifetime.

Meditation must be the immediate focus of all initiates on this path to accomplish God actualisation. Everything else is secondary. With meditation, we can extend our consciousness into supernatural dimensions and attain God actualisation.

There are five stages to meditation. The first stage is learning to still the mind. This phase can be instantaneous at the time of our initiation, or it can take a lifetime of dedicated meditation.

The second stage is when, after attaining and maintaining perfect concentration, we get to meet the luminous or Shabd form of the guru.

The third stage starts when the Shabd form of the master guides the disciple safely through the astral and causal regions. The fourth stage is self-realisation, when the soul reaches the fourth spiritual region. In joy and ecstasy, with the disciple having shed body and mind, the soul realises it is pure spirit. The soul finally remembers it and exclaims, 'What am I!'

The fifth and final stage is God actualisation, when the soul merges with the divine word, the Shabd, and all sense of duality disappears. The drop becomes one with the ocean.

94

THE VALUE OF SATSANG

Humans are endowed with extraordinary power, incomparable speed, and divine ability in the animal kingdom. However, the veil of ignorance causes many conflicts. Sorrows also arise in this state of self-forgetfulness. Therefore, for real nature realisation, unbroken joy and everlasting peace, satsang as a process of self-study is the best. Let us remind ourselves how fortunate we are to be able to attend satsang. No matter when or where followers of the spiritual path gather for satsang, it is the best path that comes loaded with benefits. At satsang, we can and should leave the world outside the door. You can describe satsang as a haven where we all face the same direction—away from the world outside and towards the masters and their teachings. It is a sanctuary where we come together to listen to the masters and their teachings at least once a week, so that we can comprehend, help create, and then absorb an environment of peace and love, which we can take away with us.

We are like wanderers, travelling through an unknown land. When we make a base in this world, it is just for the twinkling of an eye. Then we will be out again, no trace of us having been here. Hence, we should live lightly in this spiritual desert and not attempt to hoard possessions as if it is our permanent abode. We can travel together, the master beside us, sure that we are now in good company.

Satsang reminds us that this is not our true home. Though we recognise that creation operates within the will of the Creator, this is not where we wish to stay. It is an alien land for the soul that is starting to reassert itself after living many millions of lives in servitude to the mind. The soul's yearning to depart this spiritually barren place will establish itself in the minds of true seekers.

95

SPIRITUAL DEVELOPMENT

Spirituality is profoundly influenced by other aspects of well-being in our life. Exercising regularly and eating a nutrient-rich diet with vegetables and fruits remind us that we care deeply about our life and body. We should be good to ourselves. Treating ourselves with compassion is just as important as treating others well. When we experience warm and tender feelings towards ourselves, we alter our bodies and our minds. Rather than feeling worried and anxious, we feel calm, content, trusting, and secure. The beneficial effect of these positive emotions enhances our sense of curiosity, wonder, and awe — and all these feelings contribute to developing and nurturing spirituality.

Spirituality and religiosity are positive predictors of subjective well-being, which in turn affects the overall quality of our life, including our physical, social and psychological well-being. Spirituality is that part of ourselves that helps us find meaning, connectedness, and purpose in our life. It includes the practice of philosophy and religion and suggests a way of living. During difficult times, we often look for meaning and connectedness in the greater scheme of things. This helps us understand and cope with our experiences better.

~ 96 ~

THE GURU'S HELP

Saints point out that we create our bondage to creation by immersing ourselves entirely in the dense jungle of sensual pleasures. This bondage is further perpetuated by the constant outcome of our *karma* and the deep attachments we form to the physical world. The crisis appears very simple in doctrine but is impossibly difficult to avoid.

As our soul starts to recognise its detachment from God, we feel a pang and a yearning to return home. We labour to comprehend the meaning of all this, and we have little idea of how to answer this insistent call from within to return to our origins.

However, we need not fret. The guru is there to help us along this spiritual path and awaken us to our condition. He explains the inward path of discovery that leads to our actualisation and, ultimately, leads us into the presence of God.

97

CONFRONTING OBJECTIVE FACTS, NOT FEELINGS

Of all human adventures, feeling close to our guru is potentially the most fulfilling and meaningful. Yet, often, we feel a distance from him. With our endeavours to reach him, we may sometimes confront a cold stillness — a quietness so deafening that it pushes out every thought but this: that the *guru* has abandoned me. We speak to him, and it appears that no one is hearing our concerns. We feel worried and confused.

However, could we be making a mistake in thinking like this? In physical and spiritual matters, emotions and reality don't always add up. For instance, if someone handed us a cheque for a million rupees, we could throw it away because we don't believe it is real. Similarly, we could ignore the unique prospect of being with our *guru* just because we don't believe it is real or happening. In other words, what we feel is irrelevant and what matters most are objective facts, not our feelings.

~ 98 ~

NATIONALISM AND PATRIOTISM

In this globalised era, Indians are increasingly being called upon to speak and participate in global conferences and meetings. Therefore, introducing ourselves and communicating our views with a universal outlook is critical. While addressing international audiences, it is a good practice to speak on subjects of global importance. A discourteous display of nationalism could end up alienating the audience and obliging leaders from other countries to treat us in the same vein. That way, everybody will end up blowing their own trumpet rather than allowing others to relish their culture. For example, if Indians keep harping on how great and rich Indian culture is, it might trigger a competitive nationalism and pre-empt others from genuinely glorifying India.

Often people ask whether patriotism opposes universalism. I feel it does not. Though the excessive display of patriotism will obscure one's universality, the concepts of *ekatmata* and *vishwatmata* are not in conflict with *rashtreeyata*. *Rashtrabhakti* and *vishwaprem* do not contradict each other, but their skilful expression is required. It is strange but true that when our consciousness expands, the bonding with the world grows, and detachment dawns at the same time.

99

DAUGHTERS BRING HAPPINESS, PROSPERITY, FAME AND PRIDE

Our soul, the life force that allows us to live, has no gender. In the eyes of God, there is no distinction between men and women: all are pure energy, all are blessed and all are equal. Sages have always maintained that every life has value and that it is wrong to kill another being. They teach us that only God has the power to give life and take life; it is not for us to decide on God's behalf whom to protect and whom to kill.

Unfortunately, with female foeticide, because the baby is unborn and unseen, our conscience is relatively numb. Medical technology, the clinic and the professionalism of the medical team distances us from the cruelty of the act. Also, many of us find foeticide morally acceptable because we believe the soul does not enter the foetus until the end of the second trimester in the process of gestation.

Nature intended the mother's womb to be a safe place for a baby to grow. A foetus has the ability to experience pain. It is a human being in the making — the greatest of all God's creations. A foetus is a human child born in the image of God, and a child brings the promise of love.

100

WINNING AND LOSING: PERPETUAL CYCLES IN LIFE'S GAMES

Winning and losing are relative terms. There is no absolute win, so winning and losing are mental concepts tied up in the self. Perhaps being partially satisfied with oneself yet seeking to reach what exceeds our current grasp is what makes life worthwhile. Winning and losing are a part of life. They are two sides of the same coin. Winning and losing come in cycles; neither is permanent.

We are fully aware of this, yet we continue to crave victory and live in dread of losing, even though we know deep inside, that one usually follows the other.

Just as victory brings extreme emotions, so does defeat. What about the loser? We owe a great deal to the loser, for without a loser, there cannot be a winner.

↭ 101 ↭

LIFE ITSELF IS A DEITY

Do not ignore the goodness that life has to offer. There are many teachings in the scriptures about diet, purity of thought, and pure attributes. The body, mind and soul, are all part of God. Therefore, the body is not a temple of diseases, but a temple of the spirit, where life is the eternal adobe of the deity.

Srimad Bhagavad Gita (chapter 13; verse 8-12) says:

amanitvam adambhitvam ahinsa kshantir arjavam
acharyopasanam shaucham sthairyam atma-vinigrahah
indriyartheshu vairagyam anahankara eva cha
janma-mrityu-jara-vyadhi-duhkha-doshanudarshanam
asaktir anabhishvangah putra-dara-grihadishu
nityam cha sama-chittatvam ishtanishtopapattishu
mayi chananya-yogena bhaktir avyabhicharini
vivikta-desha-sevitvam aratir jana-sansadi
adhyatma-jnana-nityatvam tattva-jnanartha-darshanam
etaj jnanam iti proktam ajnanam yad ato 'nyatha

(Humbleness; freedom from hypocrisy; non-violence; forgiveness; simplicity; service of the Guru; cleanliness of body and mind; steadfastness; self-control; dispassion towards the objects of the senses; absence of egotism; keeping in mind the evils of birth, disease, old age, and death; non-attachment; absence of clinging to spouse, children, home, and so on; even-mindedness amidst desired and undesired events in life; constant and exclusive devotion toward Me; an inclination for solitary places and an aversion for mundane society; constancy in spiritual knowledge; and philosophical pursuit of the Absolute Truth all these I declare to be knowledge, and what is contrary to it, I call ignorance.)

EPILOGUE

Grace, even when it descends, is very fleeting. If we are not poised to receive it when it descends, we will escape its dimension and only be aware of it descending. It may manifest itself in many way—image, sound or both—even though we can't see or hear it. We have to be ready to receive it in a formless way. We have to be devoid of chaotic thoughts and be more interiorised.

SWAMI AVDHESHANAD GIRI

Gurudeo, as Swami Mahamandaleshwar Avdheshanand Giri is called by millions of his followers, prefers to remain reticent about himself though he earns the respect of listeners of all his regular and incidental discourses in which he does not restrain the flow of thoughts for the benefit of his listeners. He is of the view that the audience should be left to judge for themselves and that one should not 'brag' about oneself. He considers self-praise as arrogance or boastful, like having a big head.

His devotees agree that self-praise can become really annoying unless it is self-earned. They remain of the view, 'When you praise yourself, do it with an honest, infectious enthusiasm. It's okay to be proud of yourself. It's okay to have a smile on your face, a spring in your step, and pride in your voice when you share your accomplishments. In fact, others will receive it more positively if you do it with genuine humility. People love to receive words from your Ganga of knowledge and wisdom. Secondly, genuine enthusiasm is infectious. When you share something that made you happy, others become happier too'. This is precisely the case with reverend Swamiji.

Gurudeo is correct when he says that with bragging, conversely, we are talking about excessive pride which makes one give into the urge to do over-the-top showcasing of our own accomplishments, especially given our penchant for widespread self-promotion. But he has risen above all such petty thoughts.

Swami Avdheshanand Giri is Acharya Mahamandaleshwar of the **Shree Panch Dashnaam Juna Akhada**, the largest of the 13 Akhadas. It is a Shaivite Akhada following the Dashnaami Sampraday (sect) founded by Adi Shankaracharya. The Juna Akhada worships Bhagwan Dattatrey and their 52-foot high holy flag.

He is a guru to thousands and an inspiration to millions. He has initiated more than a hundred thousand sannyasis and transformed innumerable lives with his social activities.

He heads the Prabhu Premi Sangh in Haryana. Swamiji is the President of the Samanvaya Seva Trust, which has several branches in India and abroad. The trust manages the world-renowned Bharat Mata Mandir at Haridwar. He is also the President of the Hindu Dharma Acharya Sabha.

Invoking people for truth, justice, kindness, and empathy, Swamiji is working for the spiritual awakening of peoples' lives towards social responsibility, transforming them into better citizens. He encourages his followers to practise tolerance and austerity in life.

He is an orator and prolific writer, having authored several books on various aspects of Indian spiritual philosophy. In recognition of his services, he was bestowed an honorary Doctorate of Literature (D. Lit) degree by Vikram University in India in 2008.

He has chaired many international conferences for climate change, interfaith brotherhood, and on interfaith relations. He delivered the keynote address at the UNO for 'Responsible Leadership Summit' held in May 2019. Earlier, he attended the 2010 interfaith G8 Summit held at Winnipeg (Canada). He was the Keynote Speaker at the Parliament of the World's Religions in Melbourne in 2009. The same year, he attended the 'Hindu Jewish Summit' in Jerusalem. In 2008, Swamiji also participated in the Israeli Presidential Conference 'FACING TOMORROW'.

The enlightened spiritual leader, social reformer, and promoter of Vedic Wisdom advocates universal harmony and world peace is the face of Champions of Change in the field of spirituality.

A Devotee

GLOSSARY OF NON-ENGLISH WORDS

Aahuti: Oblation, sacrifice, offering to God

Abhishek: Consecration

Aparigraha: Non-possession

Arunoday: End of night when it moves towards daybreak; dawn

Asteya: Non-stealing

Atishudra: An individual belonging to any of the low classes of people beyond the divisions of Shudra

Atma/Aatmaa/Atman: Soul

Avatar: A manifestation of a deity or released soul in bodily form on earth

Brahman: The ultimate reality underlying all phenomena in the Hindu scriptures

Daan: Donation

Dharma: The basic principle of divine law in Hinduism; a code of proper conduct conforming to one's duty and nature

Ekatmata: Solidarity

Janma: Birth

Jiva: A living being

Jivatma: An individual soul

Karma: The sum of a person's good and bad actions in this and previous states of existence that affects their future

Karmana: By destiny

Karmic: Denoting good or bad luck brought on as a result of one's actions

Linga: A votary object that symbolises God Shiva and is revered as an emblem of generative power

Muhurat: Auspicious beginning

Manasa: Conceived or born in the mind, intellect, heart. It also denotes a creative person who creates with his or her mind

Mantras: Word, phrase or a prayer that is chanted or sung

Nada: Musical sound

Nam: Name

Nirguna: Without distinction

Panchakosha, Sharira-Tryam: In *Taittiriya Upanishad*, using *pancha koshas* (five layers). The *koshas* are:

1. *Annamaya Kosha*, our physical body
2. *Pranamaya Kosha* is the breath/chetna that keeps the physical body alive
3. *Manomaya Kosha*: Layer of mind, which controls the physical body
4. *Vijnanmaya Kosha*: Layer of intelligence, which learns and analyzes things, and helps us decide how to behave in various situations
5. *Anandamaya Kosha*: Layer of eternal happiness. The real self (Aatma) is hidden inside the Anandamaya Kosha

Additionally, the layers are also divided into three types of bodies:

1. *Sthula Sharir*: This is made of the Annamaya and Pranamaya Koshas, representing our physical body, which we are currently using in this life.

2. *Suksham Sharir* is made of Manomay, and Vijnanmaya Koshas. This is the controlling engine for the Sthula Sharir, and decides how we act/behave.
3. *Karan-Sharir*, made of Anandamaya Kosha. This is the reason why we are born, and it carries the karma/vasana/gunas across various birth-and-death cycles.

Paramatma: Absolute Atman, or Supreme Self

Phala: The fruit or consequence of a particular action (karma)

Prasad: A religious offering

Prema: Love/affection

Rashtrabhakti: Patriotism

Rashtriyata: Nationalism

Sadhvi: Saintly woman

Sadhana: Meditation

Samskara: A purificatory Hindu ceremony

Sant Mat: Conviction of the saints and sages

Satsang: Being in the company of Truth

Satya: The Truth

Seva: Service

Shabda: Relying on word, the testimony of past or present reliable experts

Siddhi: Knowledge, accomplishment, attainment

Simran: Meditation; remembrance; memory

Swadhyaya: Self-study and the recitation of the Vedas and other sacred texts

Sadhu: Sage

Sadhika: Woman achiever

Shashtra: An authoritative religious or scientific treatise

Shunya: Vacuum, void

Shloka: A couplet or distich of Sanskrit verse

Saguna: With attributes or with qualities

Vishwaprem: Universal charity

Vishwatmata: Universal soul

Vacha: Spoken word

Yajna: Any ritual done in front of a sacred fire, often with mantras

Yogi: A person who is proficient in yoga

Yogini: A woman who is proficient in yoga

MORE BY THE AUTHOR

Live fearlessly, like a child for whom the world is filled with endless possibilities. God loves us, no matter what religion we follow. The mysterious realms of time, nature and karma are open to human understanding. Swami Avdheshanand Giri, the spiritual head of one of India's oldest mutts, is an apostle of peace and a bringer of serenity. He has initiated thousands of sannyasis into the Juna Akhara and touched the lives of millions of others through his service to society. This book brings together 108 nuggets of wisdom from Swamiji's teachings that will help create a balance be- tween excellence in everyday life and spiritual attainment. By developing an awareness of our subconscious thoughts, he says, we can assume control over our perspectives and actions. Satisfaction comes from gratitude and recognising the blessings in our lives, which helps fight greed and the desire for excess. He advocates a simple yet passionate life, filled with love and kindness for one and all, as a way to be closer to God. This is timeless wisdom from a sage who has devoted himself to God and to the service of humanity—wisdom that will give you the power to control your thoughts and feelings, and empower you to believe in the best within you.

www.ingramcontent.com/pod-product-compliance
Lightning Source LLC
LaVergne TN
LVHW010346070526
838199LV00065B/5793